TWO-MINUTE OFFENSE FOR A WINNING MARRIAGE

TWO-MINUTE OFFENSE FOR A WINNING MARRIAGE

For Men Who Know More
About Football Than Marriage

Doug Kingsriter

Wolgemuth & Hyatt, Publishers, Inc.
Brentwood, Tennessee

The mission of Wolgemuth & Hyatt, Publishers, Inc. is to publish and distribute books that lead individuals toward:

- A personal faith in the one true God: Father, Son, and Holy Spirit;
- A lifestyle of practical discipleship; and
- A worldview that is consistent with the historic, Christian faith.

Moreover, the Company endeavors to accomplish this mission at a reasonable profit and in a manner which glorifies God and serves His Kingdom.

© 1989 by Doug Kingsriter

All rights reserved. Published October 1989. First Edition.

No part of this publication may be reproduced, stored in a retrieval system, or transmitted in any form by any means, electronic, mechanical, photocopy, recording, or otherwise, without the prior written permission of the publisher, except for brief quotations in critical reviews or articles.

Unless otherwise noted, all scripture quotations are from the Holy Bible, New International Version. © 1973, 1978, 1984 International Bible Society. Used by permission of Zondervan Bible Publishers.

Wolgemuth & Hyatt, Publishers, Inc.
1749 Mallory Lane, Suite 110, Brentwood, Tennessee 37027.
Printed in the United States of America.

Library of Congress Cataloging-in-Publication Data

Kingsriter, Doug.
    Two-minute offense for a winning marriage : for men who know more about football than marriage / Doug Kingsriter. — 1st ed.
      p. cm.
    ISBN 0-943497-59-0 : $14.95
    1. Husbands—Religious life. 2. Marriage—Religious aspects—Christianity. I. Title.
BV4843.K56 1989
248.8'425—dc20

89-27532
CIP

To my teammate, Debbie,
who stayed in the game
when the going was tough
so we could experience the happiness
of being on a winning team;

To my children, Lauren and Barrett,
who let me use the computer
to write this manuscript;

And to those husbands
who believe the struggle
for a better relationship
with their spouses
is worthwhile.

CONTENTS

Acknowledgments / ix

Introduction / 1

Part One: Game Plan for a Winning Marriage

1. The Two-Minute Offense / 7
2. The Head Coach / 15
3. A Championship Game Plan / 23
4. Who's Playing What? / 35
5. The Quarterback / 47
6. Film Sessions / 55
7. The Opposition / 63

Part Two: Plays for a Winning Marriage

8. The Mental Game / 75
9. The Will to Win / 85
10. A Big-Play Block / 95
11. A Fast Sprint to the Sauna / 103
12. A Tap in the Tunnel / 113
13. The Victory Celebration / 123

14. Hide 'n' Seek / *131*
15. "I Can't Hear You!" / *139*
16. Team Meetings / *149*
17. A Veteran's Legacy / *157*
18. The Power of Love / *165*

Part Three: Conclusion

19. The Two-Minute Offense at Work / *175*

About the Author / *179*

ACKNOWLEDGMENTS

I have immense appreciation for Ann Hibbard's generous editorial assistance, encouragement, guidance, and organizational skill during the writing of this manuscript. Her enthusiastic presentation of the Two-Minute Offense concept to Robert Wolgemuth and Michael Hyatt made this book possible.

I am indebted to S. Rickly Christian for his ever-so-skilled editing that carried this writing a quantum leap forward. His work through the night to meet deadlines was the effort of a true friend.

And special thanks to Robert and Mike, who believed in the far-fetched idea that football terminology could be applied to marriage. They have treated me like a best-selling author, for which I am most grateful.

INTRODUCTION

While watching a Sunday afternoon game last fall I thought back on my years of professional football. Suddenly the idea struck. "Debbie," I said casually, "I think marriage is like the game of football."

It seemed a straightforward enough comment, but not to her. She looked at me like a linebacker looks when you tell him the play's going the other way. "Which part?" she asked suspiciously.

Stupid me. I had made another one of those statements that was going to need *lots* of explanation. I stalled for time.

"Which part of what?"

"Which part of football is like marriage?" she pursued, turning to face me.

"You know, offense and defense," I answered with feigned confidence. "We're the offense — you and me! We're trying to win!" I said before I had any time to think. It was a quick response under pressure, just like an all-pro quarterback ducking the rush to keep the play alive.

"If we're the offense," she pressed, "then why do I feel like we're playing *against* each other more often than *with* each other?"

Debbie's question penetrated my protective system and slammed me into the turf of reality. I had to admit she was right. Having played twenty years of organized football from sandlot to Super Bowl, I knew what it was like to be on a cohesive, winning team. What was it that was causing so much defeat in our home?

As I reflected on our marriage, I had to admit that we were not working together, nor were we a winning team. The truth was, we were losing, and losing badly. The clock was seemingly ticking off the final seconds of our relationship's fourth quarter. We were in trouble.

Not knowing what to do, I searched for an answer. Couldn't my understanding of the winning dynamics of a football team help me build a strong marriage?

What does a pro quarterback do to win when his team is behind and they're running out of time? Does he walk off the field and quit? Does he admit defeat and congratulate the opposition? Does he just watch the clock run out?

No! He dumps the plays that have been unsuccessful and bursts into a two-minute offense that utilizes big-yardage plays while conserving precious time.

I remembered those two-minute drills and how we worked to get the ball into the end zone. I remembered how our all-pro quarterback Fran Tarkenton attacked the defense. Suddenly I knew I had to develop my own two-minute offense for our marriage . . . or else.

That's how this book came about and came to be titled. It is written for those of us who understand football more than we understand marriage. It's for those of us who find ourselves in need of a two-minute, hurry-up offense to save our marriages from imminent defeat.

Impossible? Think about it: How many football games have you seen where your team was destined for defeat, when an incredible turn of events gave them the victory? This happened with our championship Minnesota Vikings team time and time again, proving to us the truth of the adage that the game is never over until it's over.

So take courage! The tried and true plays in this book can help you develop a winning game plan that will enable you and your spouse to become a cohesive and powerful unit.

You can also learn why the strategies you've previously utilized in your relationship have resulted in trouble, despair, and heartache.

While I have yet to attain a perfect marriage, I've utilized the concepts in this book and have found more success than I ever thought possible! You can, too.

So keep reading. And may God help you as you work toward the goal of a winning marriage!

PART ONE

GAME PLAN FOR A WINNING MARRIAGE

1
THE TWO-MINUTE OFFENSE

It was January 27, 1989, the final minutes of Super Bowl XXIII were ticking off the clock, and the San Francisco 49er's were losing. It had been an exciting, seesaw game. The Cincinnati Bengals kicked a field goal to pull ahead sixteen to thirteen with three minutes left. The ensuing kickoff left the 49er's with the ball on their own ten-yard line, ninety yards from victory and 180 seconds from defeat. They had one hope for winning, and that was their two-minute offense. It was the only way they could gain big yardage quickly.

Tension mounted with each passing second. A crowd of seventy-five thousand people in Miami's Joe Robbie Stadium and millions more by television were full of anticipation. Everyone was wondering how quarterback Joe Montana could withstand the coronary pressure of this Super Bowl situation. His offense had stalled most of the game, and now he had to throw passes into a pouncing Bengal prevent defense that knew he had to gain thirty yards a minute.

Eleven Bengals moved onto the field like jungle cats stalking the kill. Hungry pass rushers were intent upon devouring the quarterback. Powerful linebacker forearms were tensed, ready to be thrust into every eligible receiver crossing their path. Restless defensive backs were clamoring to claw an interception that could clinch a Bengal victory.

The 49er's started their final drive. Montana took the snap and dropped behind excellent line protection. He cocked his arm and threw. Completion! Nine yards to Roger Craig. Another completion to John Frank gained six more. Jerry Rice snagged the next pass along the right sideline, stepping out of bounds to stop the clock. Craig ran twice, making critical yardage and moved the ball to the thirty-one. Two minutes left and sixty-nine yards to score.

Montana connected with Rice down the left sideline for seventeen yards. A swing pass to Craig out of the backfield gained thirteen more and another first down. The clock was running with one minute, twenty-two seconds left. The 49er's were in a no-huddle offense and scrambled to the line of scrimmage so Montana could fire the ball out of bounds to stop the clock.

The crowd was in a frenzy as the 49er's approached field goal range! But on the next play an ineligible receiver downfield cost them a ten-yard penalty and loss of a down. With forty-five yards to go and one minute left, Jerry Rice made a fantastic twenty-seven-yard catch across the middle! The ball was on the eighteen. Another pass to Craig got eight yards! First and goal on the ten with thirty-four seconds remaining! The crowd jumped to their feet as Montana barked his orders. Taking the snap, he scanned the end zone. Then he zipped a scorcher between two defenders. Wide-receiver John Harris went airborne. Touchdown!

Those who saw the finish will remember that incredible drive for a long time. It was a classic example of a winning two-minute offense that seized a stunning and memorable victory from almost certain defeat.

Game Conditions Reveal True Character

The true character of any team cannot be determined until tested in game conditions. In Super Bowl XXIII, the 49er's faced an extraordinary test. The pressure and stakes were at maximum levels, and the 49er's "heart" was on trial in those final ninety seconds.

Three possible options faced the 49er's while they huddled at their goal line and considered the difficult task of gaining the half-yard per second needed to win. They could:

- Continue with the same offensive strategy used in the first fifty-seven minutes and hope for a different outcome,

- Decide the end zone was too far and quit, or

- Stay in the game and change their strategy to meet the challenge.

Let's take a quick look at each of these options, because they're the same ones you face in your marriage.

Option One—Continue with the Same Strategy

Prior to their final drive, the 49er's gained 364 yards in just over twenty-four minutes, or about fifteen yards per minute. Utilizing the same offensive strategy would leave them forty-five yards short of the goal line when the clock ran out. Continuing with the same strategy meant certain defeat.

Option Two—Give Up

What if Joe Montana had decided that the pressure was too much? What if he had walked off the field after the team got the ball on their ten-yard line with three minutes left? His teammates would have begged, pleaded, threatened, and arm-twisted. The conversation would probably have gone something like this:

"Joe! What are you doing? There's still some time left!"

"I'm through, guys. I'm tired, and it's just too tough out there. I can't go another step."

"But Joe, this is it! This is the Super Bowl! You can't quit now! We need you!"

"You'll just have to finish without me."

"But Joe, you can't do this to your teammates!"

"Look, I've got my own life to live. I don't know why you think you can win this game — we've got too far to go."

"But Joe, how do you think we're gonna feel?"

"What do you mean you? This game's had a terrible effect on me. I'm stiff and sore. I can barely lift my arm, and my head hurts."

"But Joe, think of all the work we've done to get here!"

"I keep telling ya — I don't need this pressure. My life's gonna be a whole lot better without this."

"But Joe, the clock's running. There's only seconds left!"

"Find somebody else. I'm gonna start doing what I want, when I want to do it."

"But Joe, *you've got a contract!*"

"Contract? Talk to my attorney. I'm not going back in there!"

This may be an unlikely scenario in football, but not in marriage. While some husbands physically leave marriage, others leave emotionally because it's too painful and too much hassle to work on their relationship.

Emotional leave-taking reminds me of the knee injury I suffered my third year in the NFL. When the cast was removed, my knee was stiff and sore. Bending it sent thousands of pain messages to my brain. I pushed off with my good leg to rise or sit so I wouldn't bend the injured one. Unless I had consciously intervened with physical therapy, my muscles would have atrophied beyond their ability to rehabilitate.

Likewise, if dealing with the problems in your relationship is too painful, you'll direct your attention elsewhere. You'll take pleasure in your work, sports activities, hobbies, or friends, and let your marriage slide. This is leaving the game and will defeat your marriage.

Option Three — Change Strategy to Meet the Challenge

With three minutes remaining the 49er's had not played well enough to win. Their efforts had left them short of victory. They needed a different strategy. There were no new players who could help them win the Super Bowl, and no other outside help. The 49ers' only hope for winning was to stay on the field and perform their very best, while utilizing a new strategy.

Choosing the Right Option

Changing our relational strategy is the only way we can turn losing marriages into winning marriages. Keeping our same attitudes and behaviors will not give us a different outcome than we have now. It's unrealistic to expect that our marriage relationships will improve without making any changes. I maintained that expectation for several years, and my interactions with Debbie only got worse.

One of our patterns was a consistent loser. When conflicts arose between us, Debbie wanted to talk about our relationship and how she felt about it. I tried to minimize the conflict by saying she was overreacting. The more she'd press the issue, the more I'd discount her feelings. Other unresolved issues soon erupted, and tempers flared. We repeated this pattern over and over again.

When I'd get to my maximum toleration point, I'd go into the mule routine. I'd stop talking. That is, if the conflict couldn't be resolved my way, utilizing Option One, I'd resort to Option Two and leave the game. Unfortunately, some husbands will physically move to a different address. But many of us will just leave the game emotionally. We give up on the idea that we can ever have a happy marriage, so we withdraw.

If we're not getting what we want out of marriage, why give our spouses what they want? If we "penalize" our spouses, maybe they'll change their behavior to accommodate us.

It took a frightening experience to make me realize that I needed to learn new ways of dealing with our conflict. I knew a couple who had been embroiled in the same kind of destructive pattern years longer than we had. Craig was emotionally distant, Marilyn was sensitive and vulnerable. Craig found he could get his way if he clammed up because he knew Marilyn would cave in, just to have a husband again. Craig once boasted that he went two weeks without speaking directly to his wife. Marilyn began to believe in her own worthlessness as evidenced by her husband's responses. Tragically, she took her own life. Not all of our losing patterns will end so badly, but they take their toll.

So if maintaining the same vision of marriage is fruitless, and giving up only puts us further in the hole, then our only solution is staying and changing. Joe Montana solidified his image as a winner by staying in the Super Bowl and changing his strategy. If you want a winning team, you must make winning plays. To develop the qualities of a winner and learn how to turn challenge into triumph, you must stay in the game, no matter what.

I am convinced that the benefits gained from working on our marriage relationships are far greater than those that come from winning the Super Bowl. By staying in the game and implementing the right plays we can break our losing streak. We can achieve individual greatness and fulfillment, but we must go the distance.

Life's Greatest Game

The greatest game in life is marriage, and every husband/wife team is highly significant. All marriages have the potential for tremendous impact upon society. Yet so many husbands and wives live impoverished, repetitious, and unrewarding lives that their God-given potential for good is neutralized. Only when we see marriage as a vehicle for change and self-growth will we begin to experience the fulfillment for which we long.

Within the protective environment of a healthy marriage we have the opportunity to explore new ways of being ourselves. We can expand our capacity to love, to encourage, to challenge, to enjoy, to motivate, and to depend on each other. Leadership abilities can be sharpened, creativity nurtured, and our ideas tested. We can discover new ways to work together, as well as new skills and talents we never knew we had. We can tap into the inexhaustible energy that comes from the intimacy of complete acceptance.

But again, victory can only be attained if we stay in the game.

> *Game Plan: Make the Commitment to Stay in Your Marriage.*

Questions to Consider

1. What are ways in which you emotionally leave your marriage?

2. What are some of the reasons you have chosen this option?

2
THE HEAD COACH

I'll never forget the first time I saw Bud Grant, the famous head coach of the Minnesota Vikings. It was December, 1969 and the Vikings were at the University of Minnesota preparing for the National Football Conference Championship game. It was the only practice field available that could be accessed by a bulldozer to clear away the mountains of snow. At the time I was a college football player with the potential to be a pro, so I was very interested in how the Vikings went about preparing for a game.

There were forty players, a few assistant coaches, and a trainer or two that were participating in the practice. Everyone was focusing on their assignments. About every five minutes or so Bud would either say a word or a short phrase, then point, and the team would suddenly change what they were doing and do something else. It was incredible how everyone responded so quickly to his ever-so-slight direction. There was no question who was in charge.

Several years later, I had the opportunity to play under Bud Grant on other Minnesota Vikings Super Bowl teams. It was then that I found out why the team responded so well to his leadership.

Having been a great pro football and basketball player, he knew the game from the perspective of both player and coach. Most importantly, he spent a great deal of time observing his players during practice and games. He knew our strengths and employed them effectively in developing the game plan.

He also knew when and where there was a weakness. Bud Grant's ability to analyze why a play broke down or why a game was lost was uncanny. And in pointing out the reasons, he invariably deepened our understanding of the game and what we were trying to accomplish as a team. Such invaluable insight, gained from a winning coach, could help me understand how I could make our marriage better. For too many years I'd been relying on less-than-championship coaching within my own home.

A qualified head coach makes every difference in the world. As a professional football player, I understood that implicitly. But on the home front, I was rather slow about incorporating that basic principle. All along I had tried to obtain marital advice from "assistant coaches"—books, seminars, friends, personal experience, and my parents' role model. To my credit, at least I sought help. But in relying on assistance from the minor leagues, I was, in some cases, offered dangerous and convoluted, even abusive, models of marriage.

One such model was related to me by a husband who thought that managing marriage was like managing a horse— it was easier to loosen the reigns than to tighten them. As he told me, "If you control your wife with reins of authority you'll have a productive marriage." Another likened the husband to a "chisel" and the wife to a "rough diamond." Chisels are made from cold steel and have neither heart nor brain. How could a model like this work for people?

I acquired several books on developing better relationships written by psychologists and marriage counselors. Each offered insight and practical suggestions that would have been far more helpful years earlier. But even at that stage early in our marriage, I don't think I knew enough about either Debbie or marriage to have gotten much out of the books anyway. Back then I felt I was in no man's land. My situation was reminiscent of the wise individual who was asked the key to success in life. The response: "good judgment." "How do you get good judgment?" the seeker asked. "From experience," he responded. "Then how to you get experience?" the seeker pursued. "From bad judgment," was the sad reply.

Well, I had a lot of "experience," but I didn't have "good judgment." And with so much advice floating around, how was I to know what would or wouldn't work? Even when I looked closely at some "model" marriages, I found people more adept at hiding problems than solving them.

I knew I was following some game plan, but whose? If I needed a new coach, who would be replaced? That was an extremely important fact for me to discover, because when a football team flounders and you want to know why, you start analyzing personnel. The head coach is first on the list.

Players Play, Coaches Coach

From my experience with Bud, I knew that a winning head coach must:

- Understand the opposition,
- Know his players, and
- Know how to make them work together as a cohesive unit.

From this knowledge a strategy is created to defeat the opponent.

During the course of practice or a game, Bud would stand on the sidelines and observe the action. Occasionally, players would go to him and communicate problems they were having during the course of play. They would describe their impressions of why the play broke down, and he'd make strategic suggestions on how they could improve their performance.

But when the game whistle blows and the ball is snapped, *it is the players who are on the playing field, not the head coach.* Coaches watch from the sidelines.

Unfortunately, my approach to marriage was often from a "sidelines" perspective. When Debbie would initiate a "problem" discussion, in coach-like fashion I would relate how she could solve the problem by changing her attitude or behavior. She would then point out that the problem involved me as well. More often than not I would agree that it *did* involve me because the problem was negatively impacting our marriage. And the sooner she could solve it, the better.

I began to realize that I made a lot of coach-type statements to Debbie—statements like: "The trouble with you is . . . "; "The problem here is . . . "; "You aren't considering all the facts . . . "; "You can do better if you would . . . "; or "You've got to change your thinking. . . ." I believed if she would just follow my advice, the problems would be solved.

Football coaches never make mistakes, right? They point out the errors players make. From my perspective as coach in our marriage, there was no such thing as "our" problems; I didn't have any. Since Debbie was the one with the problems, I figured that she was the only person who could solve them.

Then an insight bomb exploded inside my head: *If we were supposed to be a team, what was I doing on the sidelines acting like a coach?*

Searching for a Head Coach

The realization that I was standing on the sidelines helped me understand why we struggled as a marriage team. Debbie didn't marry me to be coached, but to enjoy the companionship of one who, in body, mind, and spirit, would play side-by-side on the same team. The realization of that truth was a major turning point in my attitude toward our relationship.

I found out the hard way that the "husband as coach" model for marriage guaranteed failure. There was only one reasonable course of action, and that was to resign as "coach" of our marriage and hire somebody else.

But who? Who knew us, our strengths and weaknesses, our problems? Who knew marriage well enough to help straighten ours out? Who was accessible enough to give us the intensive care we needed? Who was that coach with whom we could totally entrust our future?

In my search for encouragement and guidance, I opened my Bible and turned to a Psalm that had often been a source of inspiration and encouragement throughout my life: "The Lord is close to the brokenhearted and saves those who are crushed in spirit" (Psalm 34:18). My continual relational breakdowns with Debbie and their destructive impact on our children had finally crushed me. I was desperate and ready to try just about anything that could help.

If you had asked me at any time who the coach of my marriage was, I would have answered, "God." Not only would it have been a safe, nondebatable answer, it would have been a fair representation of my personal belief system. But in actuality I had been directing my own actions and reactions toward Debbie, resulting in great discord.

I finally realized there was very little evidence that God was a consultant, let alone head coach directing my part of our marriage relationship. In honestly evaluating the "coach" question I found that, aside from church attendance, prayer before meals, some Bible reading, and a few religious seminars, I had kept God in the press box and had unplugged the headset.

The Apostle Paul refers to Christians as athletes who should strive to win the race of faith (see 1 Corinthians 9:24). That task can only be accomplished, whether individually or within marriage, by turning to God who created the master game plan for life.

All of us want God on our side because we believe in His ability to help us. But how do you retain the Almighty as the Head Coach for your marriage? The truth of the matter is that God has offered us an unconditional contract to be our coach. What we have to do is plug in the headset to reestablish contact, and then study His game plan for marriage, which He has laid out in the Bible.

God's strategy for a winning marriage is outlined in the first three chapters of Genesis as we'll see in the next chapter. He knows marriage because He designed it. Later in the Bible, Psalm 139 reveals His knowledge of us while we were still in our mother's womb. He knows our thoughts, our ways, and our words, even before we say them. Isaiah wrote that He calls us by name. And as Matthew tells us in the first Gospel, God even knows the declining number of hairs on our heads. That is, He knows everything about each player in every marriage.

But He doesn't force His strategies down our throats. Amazingly, He gives us the freedom to either follow His advice or go our own way. The choice is ours.

Decision Point

At most critical junctures in our lives, we can usually follow two divergent roads. One ultimately leads to greater resolution, the other to greater distress. I reached this point when the breakdown in our home brought me to the choice between changing my approach to marriage or changing addresses.

Perhaps you are at such a place in your relationship with your spouse. To continue doing what you have always done, yet expecting a different outcome is sheer craziness. The truth is, we cannot rely on minor league advice nor serve as coach ourselves and expect our marriages to improve. That will only happen when we turn the job over to someone greater than ourselves.

> Game Plan: I hereby resign as head coach of my marriage. I will retain God in that position and agree to follow His game plan.
>
> _____
> (Your Signature)

Questions to Consider

1. What are some ways that you act like a coach to your spouse?

2. What attributes would you look for if you could hire a coach for your marriage?

3
A CHAMPIONSHIP GAME PLAN

Half-dressed players moved around the room, talking, laughing, and extending congratulations to their teammates. Others were clowning and throwing rolls of tape at each other. The lighthearted mood was due to our latest win. It was no ordinary victory—we had just won our first play-off game the day before and were ready to start preparing for the Dallas Cowboys! The winner of that contest would go to the Super Bowl.

Jerry Burns, our offensive coordinator, strode into the room and opened his notes on the table that supported an overhead projector. He flashed a "let's get down to business" look, and we soon fell silent.

"The Dallas Cowboys are a tremendous football team," he soberly began. "We've heard all year about their Flex Defense and about how it has stopped even the best offenses. But I believe we've got an excellent game plan and have the talent in this room to beat those guys. We're gonna show everyone that we're the best team in this league!"

Everyone's eyes were on his. He had our complete attention as he continued. "I've studied these guys for weeks now, anticipating we'd have this opportunity to play them in this game. I've seen everything they do defensively and know their every weakness."

This was encouraging news. Sportswriters talked about the Cowboy's Flex Defense as if it were a garbage disposal, capable of chewing us up like carrots. Indeed, Dallas was known for allowing very few points while physically battering every team they played.

"Now I've heard all I'm gonna hear about how great they are," he said. "We don't care how great they are, or even what they're gonna do. This is what *we're* gonna do!" With that statement, he flipped on the overhead projector and proceeded to present the finest and most comprehensive offensive strategy that we had seen all year! It was absolutely championship caliber!

We'd all heard hundreds of "Win one for the Gipper!" speeches. In football you come to expect them. But Jerry's was different. It had power — a motivating power that launched our team into unified action.

After the presentation, we burst from the room with such overwhelming enthusiasm that our defensive team caught it, too. We had a plan that won the confidence of every team member. We would play like never before! We would dismantle the Cowboy garbage disposal! To us the game had already been won. It was just a matter of flying to Dallas and playing it.

To Win or Not to Win

Believing in the game plan was a conscious choice on our part. We could just as well have discounted Jerry's strategy and remarks as one more motivational speech in a long series of others. Had we done this, I'm convinced we would have excluded a key ingredient for winning that NFC championship game.

Oh, we still would have had the game plan, and I'm sure we would have executed it just as it was given. But our practices would have been mechanical and lifeless. We would have robbed ourselves of the great power that came from *unequivocally believing* in the strategy given us to implement.

In the same way we can run the risk of failing in marriage by not firmly believing in the game plan which God extended to us in Scripture. We must have faith that His plan will work! I think this is what the author of Hebrews meant in writing, "without faith it is impossible to please God" (11:6).

We must also believe in His *complete* game plan. Believing in just a part puts us back in the decision-making position of coach. Maintaining the misguided belief that we know it all leaves us powerless.

The Beginning

This same misguided belief brought conflict into the harmony God intended for marriage. Husbands and wives have been been hamstrung ever since.

The first chapters of Genesis record God's creation of Adam from dust. He said it wasn't good for him to be alone, so He made a "teammate" from one of Adam's ribs.

This creation process distinguished Adam and Eve from all other pairs of animals for two reasons: (1) they were made in the image of God, and (2) Eve was formed by God from Adam, making them, in essence, one flesh.

In the first press conference ever called (the Genesis press conference), Adam was quoted as saying:

> This is now bone of my bones
> and flesh of my flesh;
> she shall be called "woman,"
> for she was taken out of man.

God, as Head Coach of the First Marriage Team had a few words for the press, too. In speaking to Adam and Eve He was addressing all farm teams that would eventually be assembled. It was in the context of creating "one flesh" that God revealed the essence of marriage for every married couple from that day forward.

Genesis 2:24 states God's timeless game plan for marriage — a strategy designed to achieve His ultimate purpose in the creation of mankind:

> For this reason a man will leave his father and mother and be united to his wife, and they will become one flesh.

Restated, our closest relationship should be with our spouse/teammate. All other relationships, especially with parents should be relegated to less important positions. The point at which we re-prioritize our relationships to coincide with God's plan is when we begin to accomplish the "oneness" God intended for marriage. God's design for marriage is for us to be a powerful, cohesive husband/wife team, separable only by death.

Unity Versus Division

We can gain broader insight into the meaning of unity from *Roget's International Thesaurus*. It lists the following ten synonyms: accord, completeness, divine attribute, identity, indivisibility, oneness, simplicity, totality, uniformity, and wholeness. Sounds like a world-class relationship, doesn't it?

Each spouse should receive from the other all the benefits of accord, completeness, divine attribute, identity, indivisibility, oneness, simplicity, totality, uniformity, and wholeness. To have this kind of unity in your marriage is to have the blessing of God. *Anything less is not a part of God's game plan for you.*

Division came into Adam and Eve's marriage relationship when they disobeyed God's command not to eat from the tree of the knowledge of good and evil. Adam blamed Eve, she then blamed the serpent, and we've been pointing fingers at each other ever since.

Not only did Adam and Eve lose their unity with God, they also lost it with each other. When God confronted the couple with their sin, He told Eve that in addition to having increased pain in childbearing, *her desire would be to her husband.* God told Adam he'd have to work hard the rest of his life. That is, Eve's primary focus became her relationship with Adam, while his became working the ground.

Those statements by the Creator initiated a fundamental difference in Adam and Eve's motivational focus that continues to spark conflict between husbands and wives to this day. This disparity in the regard for and willingness to work on the marriage relationship creates a wedge of disharmony. Ultimately, the relationship becomes fractured. But when the desire for a balanced relationship is equally important to both spouses, the husband/wife team has the basis to create a winning marriage.

Unity and Its Result

Jerry Burns' words echoed in our minds all week before the championship game. "The more unity you have as a football team, the greater your chance to win!" Our predominant strategy for scoring against the Cowboys was to present a unified front at the point of attack. This front would "crack" their defense. Our success depended on the ability of our offense to find or create "holes" in which we could run or pass successfully.

More specifically, scoring points against the Cowboys was a matter of recognition and reaction. Offensively, we had to recognize in a split second on every play the specific defensive pattern they were employing, then react instinctively to block the right man or run the right pattern. Our individual assignments varied on each play according to which one of the myriad defensive strategies Dallas utilized. If we recognized and reacted correctly, the play would be successful. If not, the play would break down.

We had an extraordinary week of preparation. Our defensive unit simulated Dallas' Flex Defense in practice, enabling our offense to understand and perfect our assignments. Likewise, our offense ran the Dallas plays to help our defense recognize the Cowboy's passing and blocking patterns.

We constantly helped each other recognize and react to the flow of these patterns, and it was out of this unified effort that we discovered the offensive play that ultimately won the game. It was during that practice week that one of our wide receivers realized that he was beating his man on a certain zone coverage the Cowboys used. He mentioned it to quarterback Fran Tarkenton. The next day during film sessions, Fran pointed out how their safety tipped off that particular coverage with his position on the field. We also realized the Cowboys often used this coverage for specific game conditions. So during practice, Fran would call this play when he saw the safety in this vulnerable position.

The following Sunday when the big game finally arrived, we took the lead. But the Cowboys fought back and scored late in the third quarter on a magnificent Roger-Staubach-to-Drew-Pearson touchdown. We remained ahead thirteen to ten, but they were gaining momentum.

We got the ball and made a first down, then another. The next two plays we were stopped for little gain. With third and eight, Fran began his cadence when the Dallas safety shifted. Fran quickly moved to an audible, thereby changing plays on the line of scrimmage. This was the play we'd practiced all week!

Everyone had to execute their assignments perfectly. The Cowboys would never give us a second chance. Fran took the snap and dropped back. The rush was fierce, but our line forced the defenders wide enough so Fran could step into the pocket. In a flash he launched the ball as far as he could over the part of the field that had been vacated by the safety. Like

Halley's Comet, John Gilliam streaked down the field, caught the ball in stride, and galloped into the end zone. No flags! The sixty-yard touchdown gave us a ten-point lead which we held till the end of the game. Our unified effort had won a trip to the Super Bowl!

The Power of Unity

Unity creates power, whether in football, marriage, or any other endeavor. The power from this synergy is so great that we often fail to comprehend its limit. Genesis 11 recounts mankind's unified purpose in building the Tower of Babel, as well as God's assessment of mankind's unlimited potential:

> The Lord said, "If as one people speaking the same language they have begun to do this, then nothing they plan to do will be impossible for them." (v. 6)

Elsewhere in Scripture we're told the Israelites used the exponential power of unity to their advantage in battle. Deuteronomy 32:30 states, "How could one man chase a thousand, or two put ten thousand to flight . . . ?" No doubt this passage was an inspiration to Gideon and his three hundred soldiers as they prepared to do battle with tens of thousands of Midianites (see Judges 7). Gideon understood the tremendous military force that could be generated by a few soldiers united in single purpose. When yoked together, even horses have greater power as a pair than the sum of their separate strengths.

We need harmony and unity in our marriage relationships today more than ever before. There is a direct correlation between the harmony in our marriages and the strength we have to fight the pressures that threaten our marital stability. Husband/wife teams who don't pull together have only a fraction of the strength as those who do.

With the ever-increasing levels of stress permeating our lives, is it any wonder that marital separation and dissolution is at an all-time high? *Husbands and wives weakened by conflict are being split apart by the pressures of life.* Harmony in our marriages is the greatest stress-insurance we can obtain!

Prayer with Results

Have you ever asked God to help you implement His game plan for unity in your marriage? Now that's a significant prayer. All of us want our prayers answered. They're our very highest hopes and dreams! But lack of unity in our marriages is the greatest deterrent to answered prayer.

In the second chapter of Malachi, God gives the reason why He won't pay attention when we pray. "You ask, 'Why?' It is because the Lord is acting as the witness between you and the wife of your youth, because you have broken faith with her, though she is your partner, the wife of your marriage covenant" (2:14). In other words, marital disharmony puts us in a soundproof prayer room.

The Apostle Peter concurred. "Husbands, in the same way be considerate as you live with your wives, and treat them with respect as the weaker partner and as heirs with you of the gracious gift of life, *so that nothing will hinder your prayers*" (1 Peter 3:7).

Unity puts the audio back into our prayers!

Concerned for Your Children?

Unity in our marriage relationships provides an environment that inspires our children to nurture a personal relationship with their Creator and find His ultimate purpose for their lives. In *Keeping Your Teen In Touch With God,* Dr. Robert Laurent writes, "Over fifty percent of Christian teenagers will sit in church next Sunday morning. Within two years, seventy percent of them will have left the church, never to return."

Have you been perplexed why so many children of church-attending parents are dropping out of church and not returning? Within the context of unity and oneness in marriage there lies a key to understanding this pressing concern.

In Jeremiah 32:39 God said, "I will give them singleness of heart and action, so that they will always fear me for their own good and the good of their children after them." Singleness of heart and action, particularly within marriage, will have a great impact on our children and their relationship with God.

Malachi emphasized the point further. Speaking of husbands and wives he wrote, "Has not the Lord made them one? In flesh and spirit they are his. And why one? *Because he was seeking godly offspring.* So guard yourself in your spirit, and do not break faith with the wife of your youth" (Malachi 2:15).

Financial Success

God's game plan for marriage even identifies financial success as another benefit of following His prescribed strategy. In the Proverbs, Solomon shares with us his great insight into human nature. After much observation he wrote, "Marriage is a covenant with God. The unfaithful will be torn from the land" (Proverbs 2:17). Ownership of land was then and is now a fundamental key to financial success. How many times have we seen divorce tear its participants from jobs and houses? Have you paid an attorney's bill lately? Unfaithfulness in our marriage vows costs dearly.

But with unity in marriage we will not only retain the land but will experience God's blessing upon it and our family as well.

Unity at Any Price

To achieve unity in marriage, we must make an unequivocal commitment to execute with confidence every aspect of God's game plan. That is possible only when we understand His strategy and practice His directives repeatedly. Doing so enables us to stand against the fierce opposition that seeks to divide our homes. And it will sharpen our reactions to the opposition until they become instinctive.

Unity must be our focus. And wherever it's established it must be protected at all costs. And the greater the victory that unity will bring, the greater the cost will be to obtain it. But it's worth its weight in gold.

> *Game Plan: I accept responsibility for the separation that has come into my marriage. In signing below I unequivocally accept God's game plan of unity in my marriage. Furthermore, I commit myself to achieving it, no matter what the cost.*
>
> _____
> (Your Signature)

Questions to Consider

1. What might keep you from believing that God's game plan for marriage will help you?

2. Think of a few examples where you have experienced unity with your spouse. What were the elements that brought unity about?

4

WHO'S PLAYING WHAT?

"Center? You've got to be kidding!" I was totally dumbfounded by the switch in positions that University of Minnesota head football coach Murry Warmath was asking me to make. My mind flashed to our living room just nine months before when he'd told me and my parents about the great future I had as a Gopher *quarterback*. Sure there had been casual talk about the possibility of looking at other positions, but nothing was ever said about center.

Coach Warmath's proposed switch was preposterous! I had been an all-state quarterback in high school, recruited to play football at just about every major college in the nation. I was invited to make all-expense paid visits to all of these schools. On every recruiting trip I took, I was treated like royalty. Each coach told me I had a great throwing arm, confirmed by the fact that I had been offered a professional baseball contract as a pitcher! I had visualized myself becoming one of the premier college quarterbacks in the nation.

All of the collegiate coaches who had recruited me wanted me as a quarterback! And then six weeks into my freshmen season, my college coach told me he wanted me to play center—unquestionably the *worst* position in football!

It was like I was suddenly handcuffed and dragged into court where I heard the judge say, "Son, you've committed a violent crime, and we've no choice but to give you the maximum sentence allowable by law. For the next four years you will play center."

I was in shock! Players who were moved to center were never heard from again because they can't talk. They're knocked speechless! They become disoriented, incoherent, and unquotable from the constant bashing.

Coach Warmath continued his sales pitch: "You've got a nice touch with the football. I'm sure you can learn the long snap in no time." The long snap was where the upside-down center hikes the ball to the punter or place-kick holder, then gets creamed by gleeful defensive linemen.

I was losing my sanity while Coach Warmath was gathering steam to close the sale. "You'll get to handle the ball on every play," he offered. "We always take three centers with us on every trip, so you'd make the travelling squad."

I could almost hear the flight crew saying to me, "Hey you with the short neck . . . sit here!"

The truth about centers is they never catch a pass, never take a hand-off, and never see the light of day after the snap. Centers are always blamed for fumbles and stay at the bottom of the pile. That's why their bodies are full of cleat marks.

It was to this doom that my football coach was sending me. No way had I been given a fair opportunity to show my quarterback skills. It was unjust! If they had such a low opinion of my skills when I was recruited, then why didn't they tell me?

As Coach Warmath twirled his whistle over his finger, he left me with one final, outrageous thought. "Centers are first out of the huddle, so we need someone who's a leader. And we think that player is you." I pictured myself running out of the huddle and *off* the field. It was suddenly very clear to me why centers were first out of the huddle. They were trying to get away!

With that he turned and walked away. And I watched my dreams walk away with him.

In that very short, one-sided conversation, my confidence level dropped as precipitously as my hopes for a successful football career. My dreams, aspirations, and talents had become secondary to the coach's need for a center. I was completely demoralized that his only interest in me was how I could serve his purposes. *I felt betrayed, and beneath my stoic acceptance I seethed with anger.*

A Fortunate Compromise

With great reluctance I finished that fall at center, capping it off with a you'd-have-to-see-it-to-believe-it performance in the Freshmen Game. I was absolutely terrible. Each play I would snap the ball, close my eyes, and brace myself for the hit. I never knew what had happened until I got back to the huddle. I'd ask, "What happened?" and the quarterback would yell, "Shut up and listen to the play!" It was difficult to go from a position where I was thinking constantly to a position where my mind wasn't needed or even valued.

I decided I had better use my brain while I still had it, so after several series I made an agreement with the opposing team's nose tackle: I would indicate with a nod the direction in which the play was going—if he agreed not to hit me. I was such a quick learner!

In the films you could tell the precise moment the agreement had been made. It was when I stood up after snapping the ball to watch the rest of the line crash into their opponents. Finally, I could see what was happening in the game! I thought it was humorous; my coaches did not. They said my performance was the worst example of play in the history of Minnesota football.

I can laugh about it now because three years later I was named as the Associated Press' First Team All-American tight end. Murray Warmath had graciously given me the opportunity to play the position of tight end, and I made the best of it. It was an honor I would have missed had I remained at center.

Years later this "center" experience became a "central" issue in my relationship with Debbie. It helped me understand what kind of a husband I had been.

A Better Look at the Person I Married

Just about every Christmas we visit Debbie's parents in West Texas. One particular year we were engulfed in an ice storm the day we were to return home. Both the city and the airport were immobilized for three days.

Debbie and I took the opportunity to watch all the home movies that her family had made over the years. It was an illuminating experience, to say the least!

For three days I literally watched her grow up. There were birthday parties at age four; first day of school ages six to twelve; school speeches as president of the student body; representing America's youth as Miss Teenage America; receiving awards for academic achievement; and many other family and social events.

About the third day of viewing Debbie's home movies, it dawned on me that the person I was watching as a child was the same person I married — a leader, innovator, instigator, debater, and journalist. She was involved, issue oriented, and gifted. Debbie was a grown-up version of this extraordinary child I was watching on the screen.

I began to realize the extent to which her parents had nurtured her abilities, investing themselves, their time, and their money into her development. It was who she was — her talents, intelligence, kindheartedness, and attractiveness — that had totally won me over.

I remembered the major recruiting campaign I had launched to persuade her to be a teammate with me for the rest of our lives. But as soon as we were married I had tried to change her! I had attempted to alter her thoughts and values. What she felt was important, I treated as insignificant. And what I thought was important got all my attention. Her gifts and abilities were secondary to the things I wanted her to do.

It was as if Debbie was a blue-chip player, a highly sought, all-state quarterback whom I had successfully recruited during courtship. But soon after our wedding I tried to relegate her to the position of center! I had done the same thing to Debbie that Coach Warmath had done to me. I had made her abilities secondary to the function I wanted her to fulfill.

I had recruited Debbie to be a star player on my team, and she believed me. During our engagement I had talked about us and what we would accomplish together. Her expectation of marriage was that it was going to be just like our courtship—full of care and respect. I had promised to love, cherish, honor, value, and care for her. But sometime after I signed her, the recruiting attention and the value I placed on her abilities stopped.

It was in recognizing who *gave* her those abilities that I began to realize how great an error I had made. Those gifts had come from God and were known to Him while Debbie was still in her mother's womb. In discounting Debbie's gifts, I was not only devaluing her, but also the One who had given those gifts to her!

It was as if I had shaken my fist at God and said, "I don't care what talents you've given to her! They're not important. What's important is that she contributes where I want her to contribute!" The ignorance of my actions was only exceeded by the arrogance in my attitude. Why had it taken me so long to realize that I was inflicting the same injustice on her I experienced as a collegiate football player?

The Parable of the Talents

In a New Testament parable Jesus told of a master who had given three servants some money to invest before he left on a trip. One was given five coins; the second, two; the third, one. When the master returned there was an accounting. Two of the servants doubled their investment. But the servant who was given one coin buried it in the ground. He didn't even make a deposit in the bank where interest could be earned.

The two servants who doubled their master's money were given great praise and greater responsibilities. The other servant who hid the coin was severely rebuked and his money was taken away.

As in the parable, I had taken Debbie's talents and tried to bury them in the ground. I had made no effort to aid her in the further development of her abilities. Could it be that God would require an accounting of the way in which I handled the talents He had given to her?

What would I say at such an accounting? How would I respond if the Creator of the universe said to me, "I was excited about what was going to happen with the abilities I gave to Debbie. I had great hopes for her potential when she was entrusted to you. What have you done with those talents? How have you aided in their development?"

They're hard questions, but they're valid. What have you done with the abilities God has given your teammate? Have you faithfully developed them?

In retrospect, relegating Debbie to a "less-valued" status in our relationship was symptomatic of thinking I was the "coach" in our marriage. I would call the plays and tell her what I thought she should be doing.

Being a center is a lot like being a personal attendant. You organize the huddle, get the snap count, go to the line of scrimmage, hike the ball, and get buried. If you're lucky you can get out from under the pile to see where the play has gone. Otherwise, you just get up and go back to set up the huddle again. Advancing the ball is left to the skilled players. Centers are not included in decision making because they don't significantly affect the advancement of the ball.

That's why Debbie would say she felt left out. I forced her into a position (role) where she was to organize the huddle (home), get the snap count (my instructions), move to the line of scrimmage for the play (accomplish what I wanted her to accomplish), and then return to the huddle again, no questions asked. Looking back, I'm amazed she didn't transfer to another team where her skills, goals, and dreams were more highly valued.

Does any of this sound familiar to you? We have made public vows to love, honor, and cherish our teammates, but have devalued them instead. Our partner's negative reactions are a direct result of the way we have treated them and the difficult position in which we have put them.

I found that our losing marriage could be turned around when I began to gain a new perspective and appreciation for my teammate. When I realized Debbie's talents were as valuable as mine, we began to experience success in our marriage. Not only did she feel better about our life together, I did, too!

The Option Offense

I can best illustrate the change in our relationship by describing football's option offense. You may remember that when the option offense was introduced in the 1970s, it dramatically increased the yards gained and points scored by teams who perfected its dynamics. The option's main strength comes from maximizing the individual talents of two key players, the quarterback and the running back. They are utilized in tandem with each other like a team of horses.

In an option offense, the quarterback takes the snap and runs along the line of scrimmage toward the sidelines. At the same time, the running back maintains a "pitch relationship" to him. That is, no matter where the quarterback goes, the running back is in a position to receive the pitch and advance the ball.

The option's success is in pitting two offensive runners against one defensive player at the point of attack, making it difficult to stop. Two factors are key to the option's success: (1) maintaining proper relationship, and (2) choosing the right option when confronted with the opposition. Teams spend a great deal of time perfecting both elements of this offense.

The winning husband/wife relationship is very similar to the relationship between the quarterback and the running back on the option play. Husbands who implement the dynamic of the option offense into their marriage will dramatically increase the productivity of their relationship. As the partners proceed down the field of life, they'll be in a strong "two-on-one" position every time they're confronted with opposition.

Several years ago I was doing consulting work that required extensive travel. Being gone placed a heavy strain on our family, yet the financial benefits were excellent. About a month prior to the end of the contract, Debbie and I conceptualized a cassette tape series that would help children memorize Scripture with music. For several weeks we discussed the pros and cons of starting another company.

Financially we were sound, but I wasn't eager for us to spend our savings to develop an innovative product that might flop. Yet Debbie felt the benefits outweighed the risks, and so we wrestled with the decision. Eventually, we decided to go ahead with the plan.

The idea necessitated a full commitment of our respective energies and talents. It entailed research, hiring, writing, producing, manufacturing, marketing, and even some distribution. By working together, we turned the idea into a successful resource for families. This reliance on each other strengthened our marriage considerably. Debbie's instinct for people and their motivation, coupled with my planning skills, were instrumental to our success. Again and again we saw how our united effort overcame most opposition we encountered along the way.

This is the ideal for marriage—husbands and wives perfecting their "pitch" relationship; where ideas, planning, decisions, and dreams flow freely between them. When each has complete freedom to contribute their best for the marriage, they will feel fulfilled.

So Who's the Quarterback?

It will be important to some of you that the husband be identified as the quarterback in marriage. The position implies leadership because the quarterback directs the offense. To some degree this is true. Husbands do give their marriage relationship direction, but they often follow a game plan other than God's.

Recently, a friend introduced me to a group by noting that I was writing a book on marriage. As soon as I mentioned this title, one of the men said, "And the men are the quarterback, right?" From the tone of his voice and the look on his face, I suspected that his marriage was characterized by his domination over his wife. As he continued to talk, it became apparent that he was used to having his own way. The sad, almost lifeless look on his wife's face confirmed my assessment.

I have found that concern about power in our marriage keeps our focus on getting rather than giving. Self-interest does more to deter us from a winning marriage than anything else. I discuss the issue of power later in the book, but let me offer a brief foreshadow.

In football, it's the quarterback who starts the play. In the "option" model for marriage, relational plays—that is, actions and communications from one partner to another—are initiated by both husbands and wives. Who plays what position isn't as important as how the play is made.

As a husband/quarterback, I must *initiate* relational plays that make our marriage stronger. As a husband/running back, I must respond with relational plays that strengthen our marriage. The vitality of our partnership must have my complete attention as I strive for unity and togetherness rather than power.

That's why the focus of this book is on us husbands. Unfortunately, we've been poor quarterbacks in marriage. We've messed up the offense by executing bad plays that have lost yardage, caused fumbles, and given up interceptions. It's time for new plays, guys! If you're game, grab your helmets and supporters and let's get on the field!

> Game Plan: Value your spouse's God-given talents and abilities. By so doing, your team will more than double its available assets.

Questions to Consider

1. What talents and abilities have you helped to nurture in your spouse? Which ones have you suppressed?

2. What are some ways you can make your teammate feel more valuable? Ask your teammate to make a list for you.

5

THE QUARTERBACK

I hurried to the line of scrimmage. We were in a two-minute drill, and the clock was running. "Set!" Fran Tarkenton turned his head to the right side of our offense and barked, "Two, ninety-two!" Then he turned to the left, repeating the audible. "Two, ninety-two!"

My mind shot back, *Key route — beat the linebacker outside but don't bring him into the flanker's throwing lane. Watch out for the head slap. Make your move to get open late because the quarterback's reading you third.*

"Hut, hut!" The ball was snapped and I shot to the outside shoulder of the linebacker. He stayed with me, hands and elbows pushing to keep me from getting inside. *Man-to-man defensive coverage!* I could hear Fran's voice from earlier film sessions, "Get back to the middle to open the throwing lane to the flanker!"

I broke hard to the inside, out of the linebacker's grasp and into the open middle! *Turn around!* I quick stopped, and spun on my heels to find the ball a split-second from my face. *Got it!* Then, *Thud-Crunch!*

The safety's tackle stopped the play for a twelve yard gain.

"First down! First down!" Fran was yelling excitedly. "Flanker right, 84 Y, 84 Y!"

We were in a no-huddle offense, and I scrambled to line up just outside the right tackle. "Set!" I took two deep breaths. *Inside release, get the safety's attention and cut across the middle.* "Hut, hut!"

The linebacker slammed me into the defensive end. *Break away! You're delayed, cut the route short!* The safety's reaction told me the ball had been thrown. *Reception! Look for someone to block!*

Our flanker had made it to the sidelines and stepped out of bounds. The clock stopped with twenty seconds left. We were fifteen yards from the goal line. Time for two more plays!

Fran was in his element. He was the absolute best at directing a two-minute offense. He had presence of mind, a feel for the defense, complete knowledge of the game plan, and a great understanding of his players and their abilities. He made the game of football an adventure. He was a proven leader and had earned the utmost confidence of everyone.

In the huddle, Fran called out our final instructions. "We're gonna run 80 Z Post. Y, don't check for the blitz. Clear to the sidelines immediately. X, in and flag. Backs stay. If it's complete we'll call time-out. Now let's score! On two, ready . . . break."

As soon as the ball was snapped and I got into my route, I knew the defense had blown their coverage. The cornerback followed the flanker to the post, leaving me alone on the shallow sidelines. Fran spotted me immediately and fired the ball slightly up field so I could move toward the goal line. Touchdown!

Bud Grant blew his whistle. At last, the marathon practice was finally over!

I caught Fran on the way to the showers. "How'd you know I was open so quickly," I asked. I loved to ask him questions because he had such a broad understanding of the game.

"When I looked, the flanker was double-covered and I knew the cornerback had left his zone. I saw the outside linebacker drop to the curl zone, so you had to be uncovered in the flat." He always made it sound so simple.

And to Fran it was. He quarterbacked the team like a master chess player, and his mind was always several moves ahead of what was happening on the field. I had first watched Fran play when I was eleven years old and he was a rookie with the Minnesota Vikings. Now, twelve years later, here I was on the same field with him. It was a dream come true!

Attributes of a Good Quarterback

Fran made things happen on our team. He had the knack of pulling us together, no matter how tough the circumstances. When he was in the game, our whole team felt great confidence and seemed to play above our abilities.

There are four attributes he regularly exhibited that I believe made Fran a great winning quarterback and propelled him into the Hall of Fame. These attributes have a direct correlation to the husband/quarterback, and I've identified them below.

1. *He had a harmonious relationship with the coach.* There was never a time when we sensed any disagreement between Fran and Head Coach Bud Grant or Offensive Coordinator Jerry Burns. If a play came in from the sidelines, Fran ran it. If Bud wanted to talk with him during a game, Fran went right to the sidelines. There was always a direct line of communication between Fran and Bud, unhindered by ego and bonded by respect.

Their relationship was an example of unity to the rest of us. Other teams were torn apart by strife over who called the plays. Not so with Fran and Bud. They were bound for one purpose, and that was to win.

2. *He knew and followed the game plan.* Fran knew the game plan inside out, and during the game would call only

those plays that were a part of that week's strategy for winning.

If a situation presented itself that warranted a play not in that week's plan, he'd call a time out and talk it over with Jerry and Bud.

3. *He utilized his teammates' strengths effectively.* Often I would hear him say things like, "White can block that guy, no problem," or "Foreman can beat that guy on the out move." Fran constantly matched individual player's strengths against the opposition's weaknesses to gain first downs and touchdowns.

4. *He made his teammates feel valued.* Fran talked with me about my potential as a tight end, even when I was a rookie. He was instrumental in lobbying Bud and Jerry to get me into the lineup. As a result we developed a two tight end offense where I played wide receiver. He was realistic about my weaknesses and referred to them as talents not yet developed.

He treated veterans and rookies alike. His overriding objective with all his teammates was to help develop their skills. In so doing, he increased their contribution to the team.

His confidence-inspiring attributes earned him great respect as a team leader. He had an excellent vertical relationship with the head coach and followed the game plan explicitly. He maintained a personal, growth-oriented horizontal relationship with the players which was vitally instrumental to our success. Fran was not a team leader simply because he was the quarterback. He was a leader because his determination to win was evident both on and off the field.

Improvement Takes Study

Fran also learned from his mistakes. In all our games, a log was kept of every play and the situations in which they were run. Its purpose was to track the tendencies of our team and the opposition in various situations. We'd look for patterns (was our play selection predictable?), find weaknesses (plays that consistently did not work), and identify specific areas in which the team excelled. This information was invaluable for Fran because *every play had to be a conscious, specific choice designed to move the team closer to the goal line.*

The log would look something like this:

Play	Down and Distance	Field Pos.	Defense	Result
Fl. Rt. 79	3rd and 9	Our 40	Nickel	12-yd. gain
Sp. Lt. 51	1st and 10	Their 48	3–4	2-yd. gain

From the log we'd know that on third down and nine with the ball on our forty-yard line, we ran a particular pass play against five defensive backs (nickel defense). Then we ran a sweep to the left side on first down.

The Marriage Log

You can create the same kind of log to identify the tendencies of the relational plays you have with your teammate. Here's how:

For two weeks, write five interactions *initiated by you* each day with your partner. This is a log of the plays you call as a husband/quarterback. Remember that a relational play is an action or communication such as, "I said, she said," or "I did, she did." They are simply actions and reactions, statements and responses. Then list five interactions where you respond to your *teammate's initiative.*

Sample notations might look something like this:

Husband-Initiated

Setting	Time	Action Initiated	Response	Comments
Home	Evening	Let's watch TV	Whatever	No enthusiasm
Phone	Noon	Called to say hi	Thanks!	Do this more

Teammate-Initiated

Setting	Time	Action Initiated	Response	Comments
Garage	Morning	Which car are you taking	You pick!	Big smile
Shopping	Evening	Which do you like better?	Either one	Trouble

This form will help you systematize your interactions in a more useful and accessible way. As you review your relational plays, look for repetitive patterns, successes, and failures. See if you've exhibited any of the attributes of a good quarterback. You may find this process to be one of the most illuminating experiences of your life!

When I began this task, I was taken aback with how many *unconscious* acts and statements I made routinely. All too frequently, I began a conversation with an expressionless look or a frown. Debbie's most frequent question was, "Are you mad at me?" Many times, the first word with which I responded was, "No." How would I rally my teammate if she thought I was disinterested in or arbitrarily angry with her?

Examining these plays will help you see more clearly the game plan you're following for your marriage. The log can give you a base point from which you can measure improvement in the plays you call.

If we really desire a winning marriage, we must purposefully change our old patterns of behavior which have steadily guided us into a troublesome marriage to new patterns which come out of God's game plan. We have to change from unconsciously repeating the behaviors and attitudes which hurt to consciously choosing behaviors and attitudes that build unity.

Perhaps the best way to change is to review past mistakes. We also have to know what behaviors to avoid so we don't keep tripping ourselves and causing more damage. It's from this kind of painful study that we'll be able to start the greatest turnaround of our lives.

> *Game Plan:* Log daily interactions with your spouse to find the losing patterns in which you're engaging and to pinpoint winning patterns to build upon.

Questions to Consider

1. How do you exemplify the attributes of a winning quarterback in your marriage?

2. What kinds of interactions do you think your daily log will have? Write the kinds of interactions you expect to see in your daily log. After you've completed the daily log for two weeks, write what you have learned.

6
FILM SESSIONS

The day after each football game, our team spent several hours reviewing game films. By the time we reported to the film room, the coaching staff had already seen every play numerous times, made copious notes, and memorized every mistake.

After viewing these mistakes over and over, the coaches would gnash their teeth until they'd worked themselves into a wild-eyed frenzy. This emotional state peaked when our team had our "chance" to see the films.

I hated film sessions. I would rather have been the lead man on kick-off coverage and break up the wedge than sit in the dark, nervously waiting for my name to be called.

"Kingsriter!" they would yell. "You missed that block so we couldn't score! Back!" The projector would be clicked in reverse so the whole team could review my mistake.

"We're beating ourselves with mistakes like this!" our offensive coordinator would snap, beating on the screen with his pointer. "The defense doesn't even have to line up against us — they can just lie down and watch us self-destruct!"

He continued his roaring. "Kingsriter, see that? My *mother* could make a better block than that!" At this critical point it was always wise to acknowledge the comments by saying, "Yes, sir!" If you didn't, they would turn on the lights and hunt you down.

Our offensive coordinator's scrawny body would be silhouetted against the large screen, pointer in hand, so he could readily poke at the picked-on player. His brash commentary made me want to get him on the football field to see if he could block a three-hundred-pound locomotive. I visualized myself blasting from my seat in the darkness and slamming him to the floor while yelling, "Like this, coach? Can your mother block like *this*?"

"Back!" It was excruciating. By now I had sunk very low in my seat. "We can call five hundred guys tomorrow who would miss that block. We're looking for the guy who can make it. Back!" The worse the mistake, the greater the number of times we'd review it. There were times I thought I'd be cut from the team right on the spot.

It's been some time since I've had my last nightmare about film sessions, but I still cringe when someone calls me by my last name in the dark.

Damaged egos aside, the film sessions served an extremely important function for our team, showing us exactly how we played. There was no room for fuzzy recollections — it was all there in black and white. That's why they were so difficult to watch. You couldn't portray a play in a positive light when it wasn't a good play.

Game films also enabled us to see how we could improve. We could see how the defensive backfield rotated on a particular coverage and how we could have run our pass routes better to increase our completion percentage. Blocking patterns and techniques were scrutinized for any flaw that might result in a missed assignment or a broken play.

None of us enjoyed looking at our mistakes. Reviewing game films was simply a necessary discipline if we were to learn from our mistakes and thereby develop a winning football team.

Fight or Flight?

Game films may sound reasonable for football teams, but when it comes to marriage it gets a little touchy. Reviewing our frequent and repetitive relational mistakes can put us on edge. I found, however, that my commitment to a winning marriage was directly related to my commitment to review past mistakes. It's painful, but it's a sure way to gain a better understanding of your teammate and yourself. I learned that the hard way. That is, I made the mistake of saying to my teammate, "It didn't happen that way," when we discussed something I'd done that she was upset about. I quickly discovered that our spouses were born with a Full-Color, Super VHS CamCorder in their brains, complete with reverse-angle, instant replay. And you know what else? They *know* they've got that equipment! That's why it doesn't make sense to fight about their feelings toward the incident. And their feelings will grow more intense if you pretend it wasn't important, or didn't happen, and avoid talking about it.

It isn't that *we* can't remember anything, because we can. When it comes to money, business, hobbies, or sports, we've got great memories. We can probably recall hundreds of past sports plays. Why? Because sports interest us. But our spouses are primarily interested in relationships. That's why your teammate can remember the look on your face, the tone of your voice, and the exact words you said in many of your conversations.

When confronted with our teammate's hurts, many of us have followed the game plan of "fight or flight." That is, we defend ourselves by arguing with our spouse's perceptions, or else haughtily withdrawing and refusing to dignify her desire to improve the relationship. Sometimes we do both. To be frank, those are the same strategies and "plays" that have kept our team a losing one. Here's two illustrations to show more clearly how "fight or flight" prevents a stronger marriage.

Changing the Contract

Let's say, hypothetically, that the National Football League Players Association negotiates a clause in the Standard Player's Contract that allows them to yell back at the coach during film sessions. The coach would yell; the player would yell. The coach would threaten; the player would threaten. The coach would bark, "I can call five hundred guys tomorrow who can miss that block," and the player would roar, "I can call five hundred coaches tomorrow who can't win!"

Such hypothetical changes would surely result in an escalation of hostilities. Instead of agreeing on areas that needed improvement, coaches and players would staunchly defend their interpretation of the play. Instead of resolution and progress, there would be anger and dissension.

An equally absurd scenario would be that the NFL Players Association, in response to an overwhelming number of complaints, would make it no longer mandatory to attend film sessions. After the first game of the season, Bud Grant would dismiss us to our offensive and defensive film rooms, and the team would file out the door. We'd take a look at Jerry Burns' face to see what kind of a mood he was in. If it was sour we'd say, "Jerry, we're not going to watch films today and listen to your criticism. We're going to head for the lake and get in a couple of hours of fishing, instead."

I can guarantee that Burnsie would throw an absolute fit. He'd be in that film room, running the projector forward and backward, yelling at the top of his lungs. In frustration he'd throw films at the wall because the players who could correct the mistakes wouldn't be there.

After a few weeks Jerry might change tactics. He would say, "Hey, guys, come on in and we'll watch a movie together. I won't yell or embarrass anyone anymore." He might even have some tasty hor d'oeuvres waiting for us in the film room. We'd say, "No way, man. You'll get us in the room, chain the door, and yell at us like never before. We're gonna eat our hor d'oeuvres *outside* where it's safe!" Jerry would again be left alone with his projector.

These are the same kinds of gyrations our partners have experienced in trying to talk through the unhappiness and unfulfillment that has accumulated in their relationship with us. Like our hypothetical situations, the "fight or flight" approach to conflict precludes us from making the changes necessary for a winning marriage.

Meeting Conflict Head-on

There really is only one way for us to achieve a win-win situation with our partners when conflict arises, and that's to meet it head on. Conflict is like the protective wedge in front of the runner on a kickoff return. If the wedge is not knocked down, the opposition will score and we'll get farther behind. I learned all too quickly that leveling the wedge involved a sacrificing of self. My self. My very first play as a professional football player was on the kickoff coverage team. This was a new experience—I had never covered a kickoff before!

As I aligned myself with our kicker, I concentrated on my assignment. My job was to attack "the wedge"—the protective shield in front of the ball-carrier. If the wedge was broken up, my teammates could tackle the runner. Prior to this moment the wedge had consisted of four X's on a sheet of paper. But now I was facing the reality of four, three-hundred-pound linemen running together like racehorses bursting out of the gate! It suddenly occurred to me that I had to sprint down the field and crash into these "full speed steeds."

I was in a panic! My thoughts screamed, *Somebody could get hurt doing this!* A quick statistical analysis made it clear there was a far greater chance of the wedge breaking me up than me breaking it up. In that frightening moment the phrase "self-sacrifice" took on new meaning.

But for whom was I sacrificing? I was sacrificing for the team, yes, but also for me. Both would benefit from the very best effort I could make.

When conflict comes in marriage, the best way to meet it is head-on! Only our pride will be injured by acknowledging the hurt and disappointment we've caused our teammates. Admitting our mistakes is the first step toward resolving the conflict that has plagued our marriages. Just like in football film sessions, mistakes have to be discussed so we don't repeat them. Then we can learn to play more effectively.

Every Marriage Has Problems

Every marriage has kinks to work out, just like every team. Problems are nothing to be embarrassed about. They are simply areas that need work. Just because you wear the same uniform doesn't mean you'll automatically play well together. You need the right coach, game plan, and plays. You need to practice together and have film sessions. Why? Because no one person is the consummate player! We all have our shortcomings and weaknesses for which compensation must be made. That's why there's a team to begin with. None of us can do it alone! The winning team is that which best recognizes its weaknesses and utilizes its strengths.

The success of our Minnesota Vikings team that played in the Super Bowl three out of four years (1974–77) came as a direct result of our willingness to identify our problems weekly and our courage to improve those problems daily.

We carefully analyzed the strengths of our opposition and projected how they would be playing against us. And that's exactly what we need to do as we study the opposition to our marriages.

To develop plays that win, we need to learn who we're playing against. This is the same opposition that has kept us from relational touchdowns, has brought our offense to a grinding halt, and has generally made life miserable for us.

You'll need your helmet and pads for the next chapter, so put them on and let's go!

> *Game Plan: Review your relational mistakes with the intent to correct them.*

Questions to Consider

1. What keeps you from reviewing past marital mistakes?
2. How can you make your "marriage plays" more important to you?

7

THE OPPOSITION

There aren't many indignities man has created that surpass the cruelty of a football training camp. It is a sadistic collection of the worst elements of prison, interrogation, and boot camp. Somehow training camp is supposed to mold you into a championship team. Coaches perpetuate the need for training camp with campaign slogans such as, "No pain, no gain," and "When the going gets tough, the tough get going." There are thousands of others, most of which aren't printable.

The obvious reasons for training camp are to get physically, mentally, and emotionally prepared for the football season. Your body is toughened by the rigorous schedule, your mind is filled with plays and strategy, and your temperament is agitated until you develop an insatiable desire to hit somebody.

The not-so-obvious reason is to create a team that can play more as a unit. I say not-so-obvious because the activities during the six weeks maximize personal stress. They don't promote good feelings. There are three practices daily, smack in the middle of August heat spells. We'd run the same plays and practice the same drills over and over. As a lineman, I incessantly hit both animate and inanimate objects, which became indistinguishable after only a few days. My mind was dulled and my body conditioned to the point that I didn't think about or care about whether these objects had legs, or mothers and families back home. I was programmed to "seek and destroy," and I accomplished my mayhem with robot-like determination.

Along with physical hardships, emotional hardships are imposed on the players, who all have different backgrounds, personal goals, temperaments, and values. It's amazing that anyone survives! Teammates dress and undress, shower, practice, wear the same uniforms, drink from the same water pitcher, eat at the training table, have team meetings, and sleep *together*.

Some coaches carry this "togetherness" too far. My senior year in college, our new football coach actually had players sleep in the gymnasium on portable cots. It was awful. As soon as the lights went out, five guys from the defensive side of the gym (the animals) would start throwing shoes toward the offensive side. You could hear the shoes whistling through the air, but you couldn't see who threw them or where they would hit. I used two pillows that training camp, one to rest my head, the other to protect it.

Occasionally, fights broke out during practice. I remember one fight in particular that happened at the end of a very hot scrimmage. Our first team offensive guard and second team defensive tackle got into an all-out scuffle. The fight did not go well for the tackle, who wanted to be first team. In a *very* short time he was eating a *lot* of dirt. In a valiant effort to save face, the tackle jumped to his feet and yelled, "Nobody does that to me . . . nobody!" Unfortunately his helmet was turned sideways, so he was hollering through the ear hole!

Most everyone fell to the ground in fits of laughter. For weeks afterward, players turned their helmets halfway around and yelled, "Nobody!" while swinging blindly with their hands.

When these fights occurred, Coach Warmath would stop practice and launch into a little homespun chat about "saving the fight for the real opposition." Then he'd chuckle and declare his sentence for the culprits: after practice they had to soap each other down in the shower—in full view of coaches and players alike! After a soaping session with another teammate, no player ever got into a second fight.

A Soap-and-Shower Marriage

Murray Warmath's soaping solution, which he called his "harmonization technique," was an ingenious deterrent to threats that could have irreparably fragmented our team. Hard feelings between players that aren't dealt with become entrenched in a team's psyche and are extremely counterproductive to its development.

That's why Scripture warns, "Do not let the sun go down while you are still angry" (Ephesians 4:26). *Our anger builds until it becomes the driving force behind all our relational encounters, unless we successfully deal with it.* Harbored anger destroys marriages.

What would happen in your marriage if you and your teammate followed this "harmonization technique" every time you had a conflict that aroused angry feelings toward each other? "Soap therapy" could become a hot new trend! Bars of soap would become "must" gifts for newlyweds. Being sent "to the showers" would take on a whole new meaning!

Looking back on some of our stormy exchanges, I can see where a soaping session with Debbie instead of an angry response would have put us light years ahead in our relationship. She would have felt more secure if I had created a place similar to Coach Warmath's shower where we consistently resolved anger so love and tenderness could return.

Identifying the Opposition

I learned many other lessons from my much-loved Coach Warmath. Among the most important was learning the identity of our opposition. It wasn't fellow teammates. Even though we occasionally fought, we still wore the same uniform. Rather, *our opposition was anything that kept us from playing as a team.* And Coach Warmath watched for signs of divisive elements as carefully as an eagle protectively watches the nest of its young.

The same fact needs to be recognized in marriage: *our spouses are not the opposition!* They are our teammates. They desire to have a permanent relationship with us that is impervious to the stresses of life's training camp and any other divisive forces. *Opposition in marriage is anything that separates the unity of the husband/wife team.*

When we first bought furniture for our home, Debbie tried to educate me on how to make good decisions. She had grown up in a family that operated a successful retail furniture store. As a result, she had developed a designer's eye for color, style, design, and layout. I wasn't able to make those kinds of distinctions. In fact, I couldn't make any. Nevertheless, I wanted to forge ahead and fill the house. On the other hand, Debbie felt we didn't have enough information to buy everything at once and wanted to wait on certain items. I wanted to order everything at once. Against her better judgment, Debbie finally gave in to my wishes. She was afraid that not doing what I wanted would damage our relationship. She chose harmony; I chose to have my own way.

Debbie did her best to work with the furnishings we ordered, but I had taken the joy out of what should have been a happy experience. Even worse, we had to live with second-best decisions for several years.

The opposition that hurt our relationship certainly wasn't Debbie's desire to use her best judgment, because she had our best interest in mind. And it wasn't her desire to have accord with me. The opposition was my stubborn willfulness, and it caused her to question her abilities, her value to me, and my love for her.

That experience, along with others similar in nature, pushed our relationship backward.

Upon being sacked for a loss, the first thing a smart quarterback wants to know is the name, number, and position of the defensive player who nailed him. Fran Tarkenton was no exception. He questioned his players and coaches until he discovered exactly why the loss took place. He also knew how devastating a sack could be to an offensive drive. Statistics show that sacks often force punts, not only stopping the drive but causing momentum to switch to the opposing side.

The same was true of interceptions. Fran had to understand what the coverage was, where the route was run, and why he didn't see the interceptor coming into the throwing lane. He didn't want to repeat the mistake. That's why he was such a great scrambler. He knew where the pressure was coming from, and rather than carelessly throwing a ball up for an interception or taking a ten-yard loss, he'd outsmart the rush and turn the play into a gain. I can remember several times when he scrambled for more than twenty seconds to find an open receiver. Because he was such a student of the game, he repeatedly led the NFL in the lowest number of interceptions and fewest sacks.

Our marriages are also sacked and intercepted by opposing forces that break apart the unity in our homes. These formidable opponents cause big losses. *But they are not invincible!* We can beat these guys, but first we need to know who they are. When we identify these monsters we'll be able to get back on the road to a winning marriage!

The Armchair Quarterback

Imagine that you're in your favorite TV chair, about to see the football game of your life. As the announcers discuss how the teams got to the Big Game, the camera pans to the playing field, and then slowly begins to zoom. As if on an invisible conveyer belt, the field starts moving toward you. Expanding and curving, it unfurls like a giant sail until you are completely enveloped by its scene. Your carpet suddenly transforms into green astroturf, and your easy chair becomes a wooden bench on the sidelines of a stadium that has a remarkable resemblance to your living room. Beside you stands your wife, wearing a football uniform. Eyeblack darkens her cheekbones. Football cleats have replaced jogging shoes. She looks ready to play.

There's one additional peculiarity about this football field. It's in the "Marriage Zone," that place between the twilight zone and the end zone, where each player looks like his personality; where attitudes and emotions take on flesh and bones. You watch incredulously as lifelike images of uniformed character traits move onto the field with you. The opposition has finally become three-dimensional.

The announcer's voice booms over the sound system. "Introducing the front four, the defensive line . . . at end, number 81, Self-Centered!" Six feet four inches and two hundred sixty pounds of carved steel runs onto the field. Self-Centered is always the first player introduced. His massive muscles ripple like flags in a breeze. The program indicates he can bench press five times his weight.

"Playing tackle, number 85, Denial!" Denial snaps his way across the field like a rubber band. He looks about six feet tall, but when he stretches to see over the cameras, he looms to seven feet! *This guy's a rubber man*, you say to yourself.

"At the other tackle, number 83, Demand!" Two enormous fists connected to a thug run onto the field. Your wife gasps in horror and shrinks back. "You're faster than he is," you say, trying to comfort her. She springs at your neck.

"What's the matter with you?" she screams. "Those hammers are gonna pound me." The truth in her statement causes your ears to turn red.

"At end, number 87, Irritable!" The shaking ground draws your attention to a pair of feet wearing giant football cleats that leave waffle-like imprints in the turf. You're overwhelmed at the potential pain this player could inflict.

The Opposition 69

Your suddenly fragile-looking wife turns to face you. "How are we going to keep these guys out of our backfield?" she asks with a fearful glance.

You mentally check your roster. "Just wait till you see our line!" you reply with assurance. "With a little instruction, our blockers can handle these guys!"

The announcer receives the go-ahead from the program director. "Introducing the front line for the offense . . . Number 53, Virtue!" An amiable-looking player jogs onto the field. He looks good and runs well. That is, until the cheerleaders show up. One rapid double take and it's all over. He runs smack into his Head Coach and takes a headlong spill right before the cameras.

Your spouse is incredulous. "Just wait till you see our line!" she mimics. "Don't worry," you respond. "We'll get him some blinders to keep his mind on the playing field."

"Here's number 55, Confession!" There's no two ways about it. Confession is short. "He's supposed to block that tall guy?" your teammate asks with a squeak in her voice. "We'll get him some elevator shoes," you promise, nervously searching the stands for someone who might be more equipped to block.

Your team is not turning out like you thought they would. Surely you've put together a better bunch than this! These guys couldn't play in the kiddie league. But you keep up a good front, and don't let her think you're down.

The announcer booms again. "Number 63, Giving." Giving starts toward the field and promptly runs into a camera, knocking it over. His face mask has so many protective bars that he can't see anything, let alone where he's going. He's the one that has to play against Demand, whose nickname is "Fists."

"How's he gonna see through those bars to block Fists?" your teammate asks with alarm.

Come on, you're the quarterback. "Uh, he's got good ears," you respond, trying to be as resourceful as possible. But the hesitation in your voice gives you away. Now she knows you've lost it. The announcer smiles as he readies to introduce the last of the offensive line. "Number 67, Enthusiasm!" He can barely get it out without snickering, and no wonder. Enthusiasm is a one-man chamber of commerce. He promptly runs to the sidelines to sign autographs. "At least *he's* got a lot of energy!" you say optimistically.

"I haven't seen him play, yet," your spouse responds with growing irritation.

"I think we'll be just fine. I'm proud of our line."

Strategy Change

Your teammate looks stunned. "We're gonna get killed! Is this what you call a team?"

"We'll run sweeps," you shoot back. "We'll get you the ball on the outside and run around them all day." *Pretty good answer*, you say to yourself. You've always been able to get her to see things your way, though you haven't had nearly as much success lately.

The linebackers are ready to be introduced as a group. The stadium quiets as this triple-threat patiently awaits their queue like well-trained attack dogs. They look quick, strong, and extremely athletic. They appear to have the toughness to back up the defensive line and the speed to cover your pass receivers. Somehow "getting to the outside" doesn't seem quite as feasible as it did earlier.

"And now for the linebackers." The announcer's voice reverberates throughout the stadium, drawing a spontaneous roar from the crowd. You suddenly feel like fresh asphalt facing wall-to-wall steamrollers.

"Number 51, Rejection." The action-hungry crowd jeers at the unpopular player. He hollers back, "You stink, you stink." He stiff-arms reporters running toward him with tape recorders. The crowd knows he's ready to play.

"Number 52, Indifference." Grrr. Not even the roar of the crowd seems to impact this player. He carries his face around like a backpack. His Mt. Rushmore-like profile shows no expression. His eyes crinkle a little, but that's all. The only indication of his interest in playing is that he's there.

"And number 59, Insult!" The crowd spontaneously chants, "Insult, Insult, Insult." They love his name and his blitzing style of play. He has a history of hitting high and hard, frequently separating the ball carrier from the ball. Insult runs toward the camera, then veers off to slam into Indifference. He can't spark an expression, either.

You teammate's body begins to shake. She can't be *that* afraid of the opposition, can she? Granted, they look awesome. But you'll find a way to look good, you tell yourself. It is then that you see what has made your partner start to fall apart.

Three mummies with helmets and shoulder pads are sneaking across the field when they should be streaking. "Oh no!" you exclaim. They're your running backs — Companionship, Affection, and Affirmation — the hope of your offense, the salvation of your team. They look ludicrous. They are taped and bandaged so tightly they can hardly move. "Looks like they were playing hospital a little early!" a spectator yells. Apparently when your running backs saw the opposition they ran back to the dressing room to get more protective tape. A lot more.

Things aren't looking so good. But maybe there's some hope for the passing game. A few long bombs and the rush will ease up. We'll be in the lead in no time, you smile optimistically.

The Passing Game

Meanwhile, the four defensive backs have surrounded the announcer and are trying to introduce themselves over the public address system. They are the most arrogant goons you've seen in your life. Their behavior is so obnoxious that the crowd begins to boo. It takes threats from the network program director before they return to their proper places.

Microphone in hand, the announcer continues. "Here are the defensive backs for the opposition." The director must cut the camera shot away to the crowd while his assistant warns the backs not to make obscene gestures to the television audience. "Number 47, Pride. Number 48, Preoccupation. Number 42, Criticism. Number 39, Competition." The all-too-swift intros did not sit well with them, and they display their unhappiness by making ominous gestures at the receivers.

This is just about the final straw for the receivers. Wilting beneath the intimidation, this inexperienced bunch now looks more like choir boys. Their confidence shaken, Listening, Understanding, Cooperation, and Love quietly tiptoe to the camera with heads down, then quickly join their teammates on the sidelines.

Love shakes his head. Listening turns his hearing aid off to shut out the jeers. Understanding stares blankly at the stands, wondering why he ever wanted to play in the first place. Cooperation slinks away from the group and stands by himself. Having lost their enthusiasm for playing, they are receivers with no power.

"Tenacious bunch, aren't they?" your spouse replies cynically. "Sure hope you like the team you've put together. They can't even stand up to pre-game taunts!" she says, walking away stiffly.

You're in tough shape. What in the world happened to your team? All this time you thought they'd be strong and powerful, but they look more like a bunch of wimps getting ready for The Match Game instead of a football game.

To even have a prayer of a chance, you've got to discover the opposition's strategy. You've got to find ways to motivate your team to play beyond their limits.

It's the challenge of your life.

PART TWO

PLAYS FOR A WINNING MARRIAGE

8
THE MENTAL GAME

We barely made it into the play-offs my second year in the NFL. Actually, we limped. Fran Tarkenton had developed a sore arm late in the season. It worsened the closer we got to the play-offs. The ice, hot packs, whirlpools, and massages had only slowed the progression of pain. He threw fewer and fewer passes during practice. By the last game of the regular season, he stopped throwing altogether.

In our first play-off game Fran started warm-ups by throwing three-foot passes. Tucking his elbow into his side, he threw with his wrist and forearm. After a minute he stepped back. Fran maintained this careful procedure for fifteen minutes until he was ready to throw short passes in our pregame drills. Each pass sent stabs of pain through his arm. He threw as hard as he could, but the ball just didn't have its usual zip. Nevertheless, his game performance remained at an all-pro level. This was primarily due to his regimen of mental preparation.

During the preceding week Fran reviewed the patterns and tendencies of the defensive coverage by watching past game films. After many hours of study, the coverage patterns of that week's opponent were indelibly imprinted in his mind. Though he could only observe passing drills during practice, Fran ran each play mentally and selected the appropriate receiver.

The effort paid off. We won our first play-off game, then beat the Rams in the Minnesota cold for another trip to the Super Bowl.

Our Mind's Playing Field

In his book *Psycho Cybernetics*, Maxwell Maltz purports that our minds do not differentiate between actual physical practice and mental practice. His landmark experiments with basketball players and free-throw shooting substantiated his premise.

Maltz's experiment was quite simple. He had two groups of basketball players shoot one hundred free throws, recording the number of successful shots. He then instructed the first group to shoot a certain number of free throws every day. He instructed the second group to *mentally* shoot the same number each day and to envision each one going in the hoop.

Maltz periodically checked each group's progress and discovered that both groups had significant improvement. Interestingly enough, the mental group tested slightly higher than the group which actually shot free throws. The experiment gives scientific credibility to the statement, "What the mind can conceive, the body can achieve."

Jesus said, "As a man thinks in his heart, so he is." In other words, *what goes on in the secrets of our mind eventually plays out in real life.* This powerful statement has some far-reaching implications for us all. Our thoughts are amazingly progressive in nature. That is, one thought leads us to another. They can direct us step by step over a mountain or lead us into the lowest of valleys.

Nothing impacts our marriages more than our inner thoughts about our teammates. Virtuous thoughts become words and actions that can create a life of great happiness and fulfillment with our partners. Our minds are literally the practice field for our marital game plays. Well-directed thoughts can build a winning marriage.

On the other hand, self-centered thoughts do not recognize and validate the needs of our partners. The corresponding actions will be focused on satisfying ourselves, and so the companionship, emotional, and spiritual needs of our teammates will remain unmet. Under these conditions, a winning relationship is impossible.

Teams function according to the level of their togetherness, and that level is largely determined by how we think about our teammates.

❑ ❑ ❑

Virtue always fancied himself as a team leader. He was the first into the huddle, and the first out. After each play, he liked to grab the hand of another player and help him to his feet. Frequently, he'd lend a hand to an opponent, and sometimes even gave him a pat on the back. He wanted everyone to know he was an all-around good guy.

His job on each play was to block Self-Centered. He had studied Self-Centered's moves in other games and developed a lot of respect for him. Self-Centered always seemed to get what he wanted, and Virtue found himself wondering what that would be like.

It had been a relatively easy game for Virtue. Self-Centered had been stunting with other players in the defensive line and Virtue's main contact had been in helping the opposition to their feet. It was after such a play that he noticed what looked like a magazine sticking out of Self-Centered's football pants.

"Hey, what you got there?" Virtue asked.

"It's my vacation guide," Self-Centered responded with a smile. "Here, take a look."

The travel magazine was filled with photos of activities and events Virtue had always wanted to do and see. His head began to swim with excitement, and he nearly lost his balance.

"Whoa there, don't try to take it all in at once," Self-Centered said in a friendly tone. "Take your time. Look at each activity carefully. Imagine yourself doing it."

Virtue heard his quarterback calling him to the huddle. "Oh yeah, the game," he thought as he trotted back to his waiting teammates. He tried to put the guide in his shirt, but the pictures caught his eye again. *Sure looks fun*, he thought.

"On two. Ready, break!" The team broke the huddle and headed for the line of scrimmage. But when Virtue took his stance, he spotted a financial guide laying on the ground.

"If I could just spend more time making money and less time playing this stupid football game!" Virtue sighed to himself. That way he could pay for everything listed in the vacation guide.

"Hut, hut!" The ball was snapped and Self-Centered flew by Virtue to slam the quarterback for a big loss. Virtue was so absorbed in the guides that he never moved from his stance.

❑ ❑ ❑

Jerry was upset. Kathy needed the car for some meeting that night, and so he had to bounce to and from work. Come to think of it, he'd been bounced around all day. Work just hadn't been going well lately. He was losing the competitive edge on his next promotion because he couldn't spend the extra time required. His work-related social life had also been hindered. Kathy again. She always saddled him with things she considered more important but that he felt were counterproductive.

The note on the kitchen counter that morning left him cold. Pick up the kids at the Woodwards', make them dinner, and get them ready for bed. She'd be back at 8:30 from her all-important meeting. That did it. All the guys at work were going to the baseball game together while he rode the bus home to babysit.

As the clock ticked, his mind replayed instance after instance where he'd been shortchanged by Kathy. By 7:30 that evening, he felt totally taken advantage of. By eight, he was convinced he'd married the wrong person. By 8:15, Jerry was listing new wife candidates. Every one of them would be delighted to treat him with the respect he deserved.

At nine o'clock, Kathy walked in the door with a cheerful hello. She was elated over the results of her meeting and couldn't wait to share them with Jerry. She was totally unprepared for the blast-furnace greeting. Within seconds, her sparkling enthusiasm was reduced to ashes by the intensity of the heat.

❑ ❑ ❑

Virtue was stunned by the force of the football as it crashed through his guide and bounced off his chest. An overthrown pass had skipped from the turf, slamming into him on the bench. His bleary eyes could barely make out his team. He glanced at the scoreboard and tried to focus his eyes. But his vision had been blurred from his close scrutiny of the activity guide.

Looking down, he saw that the football had torn his guide in half. The pictures were crumpled and didn't look as inviting as when he first saw them. The abhorrent thought struck him that he had been tricked by Self-Centered, and he suddenly wanted to be on the field with his teammates.

His vision was still impaired, but it was clearing. Virtue rushed onto the field. "Glad to have you back—we've needed you!" his quarterback greeted him. Virtue couldn't help but notice the broken nose and black eye sustained by the quarterback in his absence from the game.

It took awhile for them to start playing well together. But slowly the team began to make yardage, and then gained ground in greater chunks. Virtue totally changed his style of play. He became very active, engaging in hand-to-hand combat with Self-Centered on every play. He earned the respect of everyone by persistently staying after his block. He regained his leadership position, and again took pride in being first out of the huddle and off the ground after each play.

❑ ❑ ❑

In no uncertain terms, Jerry let Kathy know how he felt about her, and even said she was a millstone to his career. But he didn't feel any better after blasting his wife.

She's always asking me to share my feelings, he mused. *Well, I finally did it, but she didn't like it very much.* That was an understatement. Kathy had never been so distraught.

Other scenes from the past week crept into Jerry's mind and began to undermine his rationale. Hadn't she taken the bus to work again and again? Hadn't she made sure the kids were picked up after school and taken to the Woodwards'? Wasn't her meeting about developing a family financial plan that could make their money work better?

Jerry wished he'd thought about Kathy's efforts to make their life better instead of just thinking about himself. He probably would have been more receptive when she came in. Kathy had looked excited, as if she had some really important news.

I'll just head to the bedroom, tell her I'm sorry, and ask how the meeting went, he said to himself. But as he neared the door, Kathy's sobs told him it wasn't going to be all that easy.

A Mental Game That Breaks a Team

"Out of the overflow of the heart, the mouth speaks," Jesus said. Our thoughts will surface in words and actions just as surely as the sun will rise tomorrow. This truth represents one of the most powerful tools you have to change your marital momentum, and you have total control over it! *When you focus your thoughts on the positive aspects of your teammate you will have more winning plays in your marriage.*

Conversely, by focusing on yourself you'll continue running plays that result in lost yardage, fumbles, and interceptions. The mental game in marriage can either make or break your team.

Some time ago a friend of mine came bursting into the place we were meeting. He was fifteen minutes late and fuming. He had had to feed and bathe his young children because his wife had a viral infection and a 103 degree temperature. He was put out because his plans and his schedule had been changed against his will. There had been no thought given to the fact that his wife cared for the children day-in and day-out, or that she felt terrible. What mattered was that he had been inconvenienced. As a result, she felt somewhat like a failure, but mostly she felt unloved.

How could this unfortunate scenario have been avoided? This husband could have remembered how it felt to have a high temperature and given his wife a cold pack and a back rub. He could have thought about the constant care she gave their children and let her know how much he appreciated her. He could have made her feel far more important than any appointment he had made. Focusing on himself prevented a winning thought process from taking place and resulted in a hurtful relational play.

Self-talk, those little tapes we play in our minds, plays a major part in the happiness or sorrow we experience in our marriages. Let's say you want to tell your spouse about an idea you've developed for your company. Just as she sits down to listen to your exciting story, the phone rings. It's someone she's been trying to connect with all day, and she talks with them for awhile. You think, *There she goes again. If she really cared for me she'd call them back after I've shared my brilliant idea.* Suddenly your terrific idea isn't as important as your hurt feelings, and in an angry tone, you let her know that she's offended you. Wouldn't it be better to think that she's taking care of some details so that she'll have *more* time to listen to you? Interpreting her behavior this way will give a far better chance of a good encounter when she returns from her phone call.

Another way that the mental game affects our marriages is the way in which we think of our spouses' appearance. How we assess their attractiveness in our thoughts might as well be conveyed over a public address system. They *know* if we are disapproving, disinterested, critical, or disappointed. And they suffer as a result.

Instead of comparing your teammate to another real or imaginary person, don't compare her with anyone. Focus on everything that attracted you to her. *As you practice, so you play in the game.* Her appearance as will as her countenance will reflect how you think about her.

Your thoughts are the strategic center to your marriage. Winning relationships start inside your head. Write down all the reasons you married your teammate. List her positive attributes in a notebook and carry it around with you. Think about the good things she does. Resist the temptation to dwell on your teammate's undesirable qualities.

The Apostle Paul wrote, "Finally, brothers, whatever is true, whatever is noble, whatever is right, whatever is pure, whatever is lovely, whatever is admirable—if anything is excellent or praiseworthy—think about such things. . . . And the God of peace will be with you" (Philippians 4:8, 9).

Win the mental game. In so doing, you'll develop a winning marriage!

> *The Play: Think positive thoughts about your teammate.*

Questions to Consider

1. How do you think about your spouse?
2. How have your thoughts about her affected your actions?

9

THE WILL TO WIN

I was blessed with powerful legs. They were the key to my prowess as a high school football player. Teammates and coaches frequently commented about my lower body strength. I had the legs of a workhorse and was very difficult to bring down. When I ran, the first tackler merely slowed my momentum. After a few yards, a second tackler would grab onto one of my legs and hang on, enabling a third defender to finally pull me down.

My upper body strength was a different story, however. At best I had average strength and was embarrassed about this comparative weakness. When our team lifted weights, I'd avoid many of the upper body exercises, particularly the bench press. I simply told people I didn't want to mess up the action of my throwing arm. The truth was that I didn't want others to know how weak I was. I wanted to maintain my image as a very strong player. If I got on the bench press, they would discover my secret.

I took this illusion of strength with me to college, where I was confronted even more with the reality of my weakness. All the players lifted weights. It was evident in the shower room and on the field that they had far more strength than any of the high school players with whom I'd played.

I dodged my weakness again by utilizing the "throwing arm" alibi. Quarterback's didn't need to lift. But when I was moved to the line, I lost my excuse. Either I had to confront my lack of strength or come up with another reason for not lifting weights.

The fall of my sophomore season I broke my wrist. Since I was unable to compete, I was given another year of eligibility. That winter, when I started off-season conditioning, I again skipped the bench press. I told my coach that it hurt my wrist to do those lifts, so I was off the hook.

Showdown with Truth

The next fall I was named as a tight end on the Associated Press Sophomore All-American team, and my prospect of playing professional football brightened. But the more I thought about going pro, the more I realized my upper body weakness would be a major hindrance. There's no such thing as a weak tight end in pro football. But to develop the strength I needed, I'd have to start from scratch. Not only would I have to overcome my hereditary weakness and the years I avoided weight training, I also had to overcome atrophy from wearing a cast the preceding year. And I had to do it with a sore wrist.

As we went into winter conditioning of my junior year and commenced weight lifting drills, I was faced with two basic choices. I could continue with my lame excuses, keep my pride, and thereby disqualify myself from pro football. Or I could lift weights, swallow my pride, and thereby increase my chances of playing in the NFL.

I'll never forget the day I finally faced my problem squarely. One afternoon, I told my football coach the whole story and asked for his help. He was very understanding and designed a training program just for me. He also shared an interesting insight that has influenced other areas of my life. He said there were two bench presses in our weight room that had my name on them. One was visible; the other, invisible. One was named "Progress," the other, "Pride." Exercising with the iron of Progress created real muscular strength. Exercising Pride created only the illusion of strength. He felt I needed to find a way to squeeze those two benches together so that I took pride in how much progress I made.

From that point on, I approached the weight room with a different attitude. I told my teammates that I didn't want my lack of strength to limit my play and hurt the team any longer. I asked for their help and encouragement. I started to lay down the imaginary weights of pride and pick up the real weights of progress. Was I embarrassed? Yes. Did it hurt? Yes. Did I make progress? Yes. Within that school year, I caught up to those whose strength was ranked in the bottom third of the team. And by the end of the next year, I was among the leaders on our team for upper body strength. My play improved and I received many memorable postseason honors. The upper body strength I developed in college helped me accomplish my goal of playing professional football. But I almost had to learn the hard way how pride could keep me from what I wanted most.

Excuses Cost

Each time I excused my weakness I fell further behind. As each excuse wore out, I'd create a new one. In my heart I knew I was not being honest with myself. My self-confidence began to decline right along with my self-respect.

The incredible paradox is that by covering my weakness, I was damaging myself. When I confessed my weakness, I was helped. An added benefit was that in strengthening myself, *the team became a better team!* Best of all, I regained self-respect.

This story illustrates what Solomon must have meant when he wrote, "He who conceals his sins does not prosper, but whoever confesses and renounces them finds mercy" (Proverbs 28:13).

Confession of our faults and limitations within marriage is a very freeing experience. It releases us from wasting a lot of time and energy denying our imperfections. It saves us from having to convince everyone how good we are. It spares us the embarrassment that comes when our shortcomings are discovered.

Much of the early conflict in my marriage came from my underdeveloped ability to love and value Debbie. And if she ever brought the subject up, I became indignant. I didn't want to talk about it. I denied there was a very serious communication problem that was hurting her. The more she pursued solutions, the more I denied I'd done anything wrong. Thus, I inflicted injury upon injury.

❏ ❏ ❏

Denial took some sticky tape from his roll and slapped it across Confession's mouth. Unable to believe the referee didn't call an encroachment penalty, Confession struggled to remove the tape. Too late! The quarterback was already into his cadence. Denial smiled slyly and slithered smoothly into his rush with Selfishness. Confession tried as hard as he could to alert the line to the blocking change but could only muster a few inaudible grunts.

At the snap of the ball, Confession scrambled to cover the stunt but was unable to get there in time. Denial's long arms had already grabbed the runner, dropping him for a five-yard loss.

❏ ❏ ❏

"What is it about you that expects me to keep working day after day without any appreciation?" Melissa asked with the usual edge in her voice.

"I do appreciate you," Dan responded, his body automatically tensing for conflict.

"But you never tell me!" She grit her teeth on the "never" as if her incisors were crunching her husband's finger.

Dan shook his head. He could never figure out where Melissa was coming from. "C'mon Melissa. I don't know what you're talking about."

It was like trying to break a brick with a toothpick. Melissa instinctively reached for a bigger stick. "You don't know what I'm talking about?" she screamed. "It's only the biggest disappointment of my life!"

"So it's the 'I'm-the-biggest-disappointment' routine again." She was always telling him what a failure he was as a husband, and he was tired of it. He'd listened to that script more times than he wanted to remember.

Dan picked up his coffee and headed for the garage. "I can never hear what you're talking about 'cause you're always screaming," he muttered as he withdrew from the room.

❏ ❏ ❏

It was second and fifteen. Confession was trying to pull the tape from his mouth, but the stickum tore his skin when he tugged on the corner. The other players in the huddle looked sympathetic but were helpless. Confession would have to deal with it himself.

As they broke the huddle, he could see Denial getting more tape. Confession was suddenly furious that such childish trickery had caused the team to lose yardage. With a muffled yell he ripped the tape from his mouth and shouted the infraction to the referee. Denial dropped his tape and snickered while taking his stance. They both expected a dog-fight.

They were going to run an off-tackle slant right over his block! Confession called out the blocking assignments. He would take Denial himself. At the snap, he ripped into Denial's chest with his helmet and forearms, making him recoil at the shock. Confession followed with another hit that made Denial's long body shudder and crumple. The swoosh behind his ear told Confession the ball-carrier had made it through the line. They were moving the ball again!

❑ ❑ ❑

Dan stopped himself in the doorway. Another failed attempt to communicate. He couldn't figure whether her real disappointment was *him* or some action he was neglecting. There was a significant distinction between those two thoughts. In a brief moment of truthfulness, he admitted to himself he wasn't giving her what she wanted. She just wasn't happy anymore. If he could just put his finger on what it was! Well, he shrugged, only one way to find out.

"Melissa." It was the way he said her name that made her stop. It was very different from his usual addresses, almost like a friendly beckoning.

"Yes?" she sounded with a hopeful note.

"Melissa, I don't know how to tell you this, but I'm going to try. I know I haven't been giving you the love and appreciation you need, and it's caused a lot of problems between us. I love you, but I don't always know how to show it. Most of the time I don't even think about it. Not very good, huh?"

The tension in her face eased just a bit at his sincere attempt to communicate. "We can make our relationship better if we work on it together," she said, slightly amused at the slogan-like phrase that had communicated her heart's desire.

"Maybe we can," he said as he reached out to take her hand. It was a good feeling to have a positive encounter after so many yelling matches. "I know we can."

Stonewalled by Denial

Debbie's attempts to help me "see" the problems that caused our relationship to disintegrate met with little success. I couldn't accept that she felt unloved much of the time. I didn't think I was that bad a husband. I couldn't "see" her feelings, so I denied their existence. I chose to have Pride in our relationship rather than Progress until I realized how it was affecting me.

During the years I played pro football, my off-season workout consisted of a daily two-mile warm-up, five quick four-forty's, and ten 120-yard sprints. Then I'd work on specific pass routes and run them until my legs wouldn't go where my mind directed them.

I began to notice that I was having days where I could only complete two-thirds of the workout. It concerned me, and soon I discovered that Debbie and I had had trouble on days I couldn't complete my regimen. My output was handicapped one-third every time we were at odds!

I could no longer deny our relationship was hurting us both. For the first time, I understood how distraught Debbie felt when I wouldn't acknowledge that my actions hurt her. She was handicapped by unmet relational needs in the same way my workouts were by disagreements.

Though it was awkward, I started talking to Debbie about what she needed from me to be happier. It was a new start for us, and she began to feel like she was finally being heard. As I admitted that the way I related to her needed dramatic changes, we started to make progress. Each time I confessed my shortcomings I gained awareness of how I could love her more. Doing so was evidence that I valued her feelings and our relationship.

It is always a winning play when you confess that you have done wrong or hurt another person. This is especially true with your teammate. By doing this, you acknowledge that her perspective and feelings are valid and worthy of recognition. It is here that forgiveness and understanding can take place. Confession makes forgiveness possible.

Consider the alternative. Without confession, your teammate is forced to push her feelings aside and go on with her life. But her feelings get more intense and become more difficult to keep in. Lashing out gets easier with each event. Confession of wrongdoing can stop these negative cycles from occurring. It will begin to reestablish mutual respect in your relationship.

Confession Drills

You'll need lots of practice, because confessing your shortcomings is not an instinct. You'll have to leave the bench press of pride and get on the bench press of progress. Will it be hard? Yes! Will it hurt? Yes, but only your pride.

Here's what you can do. Take responsibility for the problems that are occurring or have already occurred in your relationship. Put them on your chest, just as if you're doing a bench press. Lift them off by apologizing. Say, "I'm sorry that I didn't . . . ," "I'm sorry that I don't . . . ," or "I'm sorry that I haven't. . . ."

See how many of the difficulties in your relationship you can find that have been your fault. Contrary to what you might think, Confession will enable you to make big gains. When Confession makes his block, you can't lose!

You won't be alone in your confession for long. Taking the first step in acknowledging your shortcomings to your teammate will trigger a reciprocal action from her. Love provokes love, and that's straight from God's strategy for a winning marriage!

> *The Play:* When confronted with unloving actions and words by your spouse, confess your shortcomings.

Questions to Consider

1. What are the ways you exercise pride instead of progress in your marriage?

2. Identify times when you have confessed your shortcomings to your spouse. What impact did that have on your relationship?

10

A BIG-PLAY BLOCK

One of the Vikings' best, big-gainer plays was the flanker reverse. When successfully run, it revitalized a struggling offense. We loved to pop it on teams when they least expected it. The more we surprised the opposition, the more yardage we gained.

Like any big-yardage play, the flanker reverse had its limitations. It had to be carefully set up with off-tackle slants and halfback sweeps. This was so the defensive backs would leave their zones and pursue the ball-carrier, giving our flanker a field in which to run. If the halfback-to-flanker exchange was successful, the flanker's only obstacle was the cornerback. If he left his zone to pursue the halfback, we'd have a big-gainer.

One day during films, Fran pointed out that he could become a lead blocker on the play. If he continued moving after the hand-off he could block the cornerback. Everyone laughed because blocking was not his forte. He might as well throw himself to the lions. Most teams made great efforts to keep their quarterback from contact for fear of injury. An injured quarterback could mean a disastrous season.

During that week of practice we had a lot of fun with Fran's idea. He would hand off to Chuck Foreman, who in turn would hand off to John Gilliam, our flanker. Gilliam would yell, "Where's my lead blocker?" and Fran would suddenly sprint down field and throw a crushing block on a blade of grass.

Later in the week, the line presented Fran with a huge set of shoulder pads. They said he could slip over to the sidelines and put them on just before running the play. Fran wore them to practice that day and looked hysterical.

Game day arrived and we were surprised to be in a closer contest than anticipated. Inching our way down field, we needed a big play. The reverse was called. The hand-offs were executed flawlessly, but the cornerback didn't follow pursuit. He had stayed in his zone and was in a position to make a tackle for a big loss.

I don't know who was more shocked at what happened next—the team, the cornerback, or John Gilliam. Fran came out of the blue and almost tackled the startled cornerback, enabling Gilliam to sprint down the sidelines to the five-yard line. Our players erupted with laughter and applause for the beaming Fran Tarkenton. While the crowd cheered for Gilliam, we congratulated Fran.

One act of giving can prompt a chain reaction of good events. In the case of our flanker reverse, Fran's block changed the course of the whole game. The seeming insignificance of one block didn't keep him from executing it, and to the best of his ability.

Fran's philosophy of football was to do whatever you can to make each play successful. That's why he was so respected as a leader. He always gave, even at personal risk.

Giving Has Impressive Results

Giving creates good will. At the same time it dispels hurt and anger. A few years ago, a pastor was accused of mishandling a delicate problem by a personal friend in his congregation. The pastor suffered quietly and ultimately left the church for a teaching position in another state.

Within the year, his friend realized he was mistaken, and by letter asked his forgiveness. It was graciously granted. The friend then helped several of the pastor's children find excellent jobs. Later, he purchased a new car and drove it to the pastor's residence. When he left, he handed the keys to his former pastor and flew home. Do you think the friend wanted a restoration of the relationship? Absolutely! And he followed through on his good intentions with the gifts that he gave.

❑ ❑ ❑

Giving was afraid. Demand was known to drive offensive linemen into the turf with his watermelon-sized fists. "They ought to outlaw that pile driver from the game," Giving lamented. He had already lost an inch in height just thinking about the pounding he would take. That's when the idea of an impenetrable steel facemask hit him. With a little help from the equipment manager and a local welder, Giving's mask was completed in no time.

"I'd like to see 'Fists' try to hurt me now," Giving's voice echoed inside his helmet. "He'll ruin those hammers before the end of the first quarter."

The running backs weren't quite so sure. "How are you gonna see through all that steel to block him?" But Giving let the comment pass.

On the field, Giving had a hard time finding the rest of his teammates. He wandered over to the stands where a contingent of local Knights of Columbus stood and saluted him. He looked like Don Quixote with pads and a jersey.

"Somebody give that jouster a horse!" laughed Demand. He couldn't wait to play against a guard who needed a Seeing Eye dog.

It wasn't until Giving ran smack into the band's lead saxophone player that he realized he'd become a comical part of the pregame show. So he took his helmet off, but was nearly blinded by the light.

❏ ❏ ❏

Rick and Lana usually got along pretty well, at least that's what their friends thought. They were active socially, chatty, and fun to be around. But inside Rick and Lana's home lived a different couple than the one the public knew. Behind closed doors, their relationship invariably changed from chatty and happy to catty and snappy. As a result, they went out as much as possible. That way they could avoid "the pit," as Rick called it.

Rick began his usual lament as soon as the garage door opened. "Ted and Anne are really getting tired of having us over all the time without us reciprocating."

"Why don't you invite them over?" Lana asked, looking in her purse for the house key.

"You know we can't invite them over until the house is cleaned!" Rick shot back angrily.

"I'll tell you one more time, Rick. I'm done picking up after you. I'm not going to be your personal maid any longer." Lana's tone was cold. Long gone was the tenderness that had been her trademark in the early years of marriage. Rick's refusal to participate in domestic chores had convinced Lana that he didn't love her. At work she was an accountant, but at home she felt like a maid. One day Lana decided she'd had enough of the maid's job, and quit.

Rick's subsequent accusations that Lana was a terrible wife convinced her their marriage was a sham. His idea of a wife was a "maid and date on demand," and she was prepared to quit that, too. It was painful but clear that his "love" was contingent upon her domestic contributions.

As Rick entered the back door, he felt he could no longer tolerate Lana's refusal to comply with his demands. And so he decided to activate his plan to move out until she cleaned the house.

❏ ❏ ❏

The equipment manager had replaced the steel mask with Giving's old face mask. By the middle of the second quarter, the relentless blows from Demand's fists had pretty well trashed both helmet and face mask. Giving was starting to look faint, and an equipment time-out was called by the referee.

The trainer stuck an ammonia capsule into Giving's nostrils while his helmet was worked on for the third time that day. "Coach says to use your hands to deflect those blasted fists," the trainer whispered in Giving's ear.

The ammonia was clearing his head. "I'll try," Giving replied wearily.

As Giving broke the huddle he repeated the coach's instructions. "Use your hands . . . use your hands." The thought gave him a sense of power that he hadn't had before. I can beat this guy, he thought.

At the snap of the ball, Demand's right fist fell from the sky with the speed of a meteor. But Giving's left hand deflected the blow, sending Demand's fist crashing into his own thigh. With a yelp of excruciating pain he crumpled to the ground, and Giving smiled as the ball-carrier galloped past.

❑ ❑ ❑

Rick immediately headed to the bedroom to start packing. "Ten minutes and I'm outta here!" he muttered as he stomped through the house. His favorite shirt and sweater caught his eye. They were lying on the chair next to the chest. On the floor were his pants from two days ago.

"Must be doing the right thing," he said defiantly. "Everything I need is right here." He kicked up several socks and his pajamas on his way to the underwear drawer. Packing was a breeze. He wondered why Lana had always made such a big deal about it. *Unless she changes, this marriage is over*, he promised himself.

Rick gathered his clothes and began folding them on the bed. They were pretty wrinkled. *Wouldn't it be ironic if he asked her to iron them so he could leave?* he mused. *She could even carry the suitcase to the car,* he thought.

That reminded him of their last trip together when he was in the car honking while she carried out both suitcases. At the time, he was very concerned about getting to the airport. But now he was just a little embarrassed. Maybe he had been a little too demanding.

"What are you doing?" Lana's voice interrupted his thoughts like a breaker on a CB channel.

"I'm . . . I'm folding my clothes," Rick responded sheepishly. He intentionally hid his plans. He wanted to announce his departure more dramatically.

Lana was at a loss for words. She went to the bed and picked up his hastily folded pants, smoothed them, and then hung them evenly on a hanger.

Rick's mind was swirling. *Does she know I'm leaving and wants me to stay?* His inquisitive look drew a response. "Just thought I'd pick things up with you," Lana said softly.

It had been a long time since he'd heard a kind word from Lana. Her "with you" seemed to make a connection with another thought that had troubled him earlier. Things he could do to make their home a better place to live began to run through his mind. Maybe there was hope after all . . . .

A "Hands On" Concept

Contrary to popular belief, women were not born to clean toilets. Neither were men. But both were born into a world where toilets must be cleaned. So must clothes, kitchens, floors, showers, closets, and anything else that collects dust or dirt. Toilets that need cleaning symbolize all the tasks that no one wants to do. They are the cornerback that needs to be blocked before a big gain can be made.

Many husbands feel it is beneath their dignity to clean the homes in which they live, just as some quarterbacks feel they are above making a block. But if you really want to make a play that goes for big yardage in your marriage, try scrubbing the kitchen floor. Or do anything else that will surprise your teammate if *you* do it.

The disciples of Jesus were astounded when he washed their feet. He got on his hands and knees, performing one of the most humbling of all tasks. He promised his disciples that if they, too, would give of themselves in this unselfish way, they would be blessed.

Giving in ways we haven't given before will bring blessing to our marriages. In these selfless acts are the beginnings of a new and vibrant relationship with your partner.

The Flanker Reverse of Marriage

Husbands, here's your flanker reverse play, and it's already set up for you! You've spent years making sure you had your own way. Now you're in perfect position for the surprise reverse! If you've said "I will never clean toilets!" start cleaning them, with a smile. Tell yourself you can't get enough of cleaning toilets. You love to clean them. You don't want your teammate getting her beautiful hands scuzzed up because she is too valuable!

Get on your hands and knees and give, guys! Put these plays in your game plan and call them frequently. Your giving will be returned to you many times over. And that's straight from the Coach!

> *The Play:* Give in ways you've previously refused to give.

Questions to Consider

1. What are ten things you can do that will pleasantly surprise your mate?

2. What has kept you from doing these things in the past?

11

A FAST SPRINT TO THE SAUNA

We had a guard named Chuck "Goody" Goodrum who hailed from Florida. Prior to signing with the Vikings, his farthest trip north was to Atlanta. He was a southern player who had an infinite tolerance for hot weather and humidity. I was a different story. To me, football was best played when there was a nip in the air. I preferred weather in the thirty- to fifty-degree range when you'd get that cool-and-warm hot fudge sundae feeling. Whenever we played in Florida, I thought I would die. Our line coach would come over to the bench where I was gasping for air and holler, "Get this boy some oxygen!"

Long about October when the weather cooled down, I felt more comfortable. But that's about the time Goody started feeling worse. To him, the coming of winter was like an ever-tightening straightjacket. By Thanksgiving Goody would have nightmares about snowdrifts in his room and wake up shivering. This was also the time of year that Bud Grant would tell his Eskimo story. It was his explanation of why he wouldn't allow heaters at practice or on the sidelines during games. All the other teams had enough charcoal pits to barbecue hamburgers for the whole crowd, but not us. His reasoning went like this:

After World War II the United States was afraid the Russians would invade us over the Arctic Circle. The job of building an early-warning-defense system was given to the army, but they soon fell way behind schedule due to the cold. Army personnel driving bulldozers in minus sixty-degree temperature could only stay outside for two minutes before having to come in to warm up. However, the army found that Eskimos could stay on the tractors for twenty minutes before seeking shelter. In typical army fashion, they shipped several Eskimos to Washington D.C. to measure their skin thickness, analyze their blood, and study their fat. The findings proved conclusively that the Eskimos were no different from army personnel. So why could the Eskimos stay out so long? When asked that question, the Eskimos said it was a matter of mind-set. They said they knew they'd be cold and tried to stay out as long as they could. The army personnel, however, wanted to be warm. Because that was impossible outside, they gave in after two minutes. Simply put, the mental attitude of the bulldozer operator was the critical factor.

Bud said that when fair-weather teams played in Minnesota they expected to stay as warm as possible, so they turned their heaters on high. On the other hand, we knew we would be cold for two hours. We could therefore concentrate on the game while the opposition focused on staying warm. As a result we won just about every cold game I can remember.

But Goody never bought the story. He said the Eskimos weren't smart enough to get out of the Arctic and move to Florida. He told Bud that the Eskimos who went to Washington should have run for it when they had the chance. At practice, Goody wore several pairs of thermal underwear and gloves, numerous sweatshirts, and as many socks as he could get on his feet and still fit into his cleats. He shivered throughout practice, complaining that the legislature should dome the entire state. His movements were like cold molasses. But when practice ended, he'd give a yelp and sprint for the sauna where he would sit for thirty minutes or more, still clothed in all his equipment, thermal underwear, gloves, and socks. When Goody was warm, he was one of the most delightful individuals you'd ever want to meet. But when he was cold, he was the most irritable person in town.

I see some of myself in Goody. When I'm doing what I want to do, I'm very enthusiastic and fun to be with. When I'm not, I can be so irritable that mules would find me poor company.

One Saturday I realized what my selfishness was doing to our family. I was trying to get Debbie and the children to tell me where they wanted to go and what they wanted to do. No one would venture an opinion or even a suggestion. They merely said, "Whatever you want to do, Dad." They were afraid that if we did something I didn't want to do, my mood would ruin the day.

The Messages of Enthusiasm

The things we express enthusiasm for convey definite messages to our partners and families. If we show excitement about playing baseball with our sons, but dismay over attending a piano recital with our daughters, we let our family know what we value and why. From experience I can tell you that our children's development is largely determined by the enthusiasm we show for them and their interests. Parental enthusiasm can fuel a child's abilities, while a lack of excitement can destroy even the highest dreams.

Enthusiasm is a powerful communicator in marriage. Our teammates will make extreme sacrifices in their attempts to build a healthy marriage with us. But if our enthusiasm is determined by our selfish motives, our partner's trust will be seriously damaged. Selfishness encourages separation. And where separation begins, cohesiveness ends.

Enthusiasm can make a major difference in restoring trust to our marriages. Channeled correctly, enthusiasm can invigorate life in ways you never thought possible. Enthusiasm is the play that can help your team make big yardage toward a winning marriage!

❏ ❏ ❏

Enthusiasm loved to have the ball run to his side of the line. He revelled in the action. And when he was in the center of things, no one was a better blocker. This was a well-known fact on the team, and on the surface seemed like a strength. "Run the ball my way," Enthusiasm would say. "I'll make the block that'll gain yardage." And a high percentage of the time he did.

But this strategy posed a problem. The team couldn't always run the ball in his direction. The defense could overshift and foil the play, so the ball sometimes had to be run to the other side. It kept the defense honest and gave other players a chance to contribute to the team.

This is the point where Enthusiasm moped. If the play was called to the other side, he would sulk to the line of scrimmage. He wanted everyone to know about his displeasure. The trouble was, the opposition knew it, too. They would carefully watch him when he left the huddle. When Enthusiasm hustled to the line, they knew the play was coming to his side. But when he dragged himself to the line, they knew the play was going the opposite way. His teammates were aware that Enthusiasm was giving away the play but didn't talk with him about it. They were afraid he'd get upset, sulk, or quit altogether.

❏ ❏ ❏

"Hey, the boat show's at the convention center Saturday!" Dave exclaimed as he read the newspaper. "All the major manufacturers are displaying their new lines. I gotta get down there first thing."

A Fast Sprint to the Sauna

"How long do you think it'll take to see everything?" Jenny asked as she looked up from studying her sales manual.

"Oh, all day. There'll be hundreds of boats with all the newest features." Dave's eyes were shining. As a kid, he used to dream about being a cruise ship captain.

Jenny's eyes were fixated on Dave's face. "I had kind of hoped we could spend some time looking for a business suit for me. I've got my first presentation next week and I want to make a good impression."

"Can't you do that by yourself? I mean, what do I know about women's clothes?" said Dave, feeling slightly irritated at Jenny's proposed imposition on his Saturday plans. "Besides, isn't that what they pay salespeople for — to help you find what you want?"

"If my life were more important to you, you'd try to help instead of always thinking about yourself!" Jenny fired back.

Negotiate fast, Dave thought, *or it'll be all-out war*. "Okay, okay. How 'bout if we shop in the morning and go to the boat show in the afternoon?"

Jenny took a moment to let the proposal sink in. If they hurried they could get to the major stores and see what there was. "Okay," she said. "But no boats until I find the right suit."

Dave felt that in two hours they could buy a suit, leaving them with six hours at the boat show. But he was bothered to think he had to compromise at all.

❑ ❑ ❑

The halftime statistics were extremely insightful. The majority of plays run to the right gained yardage. Enthusiasm beamed with pride. Surely he was responsible for this impressive statistic. Plays run to the left all lost yardage. The press box coach reported that on plays run to the left, the opposition got to the point of attack before the offense.

"I think it has something to do with me, Coach," Enthusiasm volunteered. *They've finally figured out who's doing the blocking around here,* his mind added as he waited expectantly for the coach's response.

"I think you're right," the coach replied. "You're telegraphing the play to the opposition as soon as you leave the huddle."

Enthusiasm could hardly believe his ears! Instead of a pat on the back he was hearing words that made him sound like a traitor. He was stunned. Silently the head coach moved toward him, put his arm on his shoulders, and drew him aside. Enthusiasm didn't say a word. The surprise turn of events had left him speechless. No one could hear what the coach was saying, but when Enthusiasm returned he had a troubled look in his eyes.

Upon breaking the huddle for the first play of the second half Enthusiasm walked halfheartedly to the line of scrimmage and sighed as he put his hand in the turf. Irritable's snicker sounded "hyenic." He prepared to sprint to the far side at the snap of the ball. But he never got there. What ensued could best be described as a herd of buffalo stampeding across the plain, trampling everything in their path. Irritable and his friends were stomped so severely that they had to call two time-outs in a row to restore the feeling in their legs.

Enthusiasm's contagious laughter could be heard everywhere. The play had worked perfectly for a big gain!

❑ ❑ ❑

After the first hour of shopping, Dave alternated looking at his watch and peering out the window. Cars were pouring into the convention center parking ramps. *Hurry up!* his mind screamed to Jenny as she carried four more suits into the dressing room. Within the first hour, Dave felt his blood pressure rise. He resorted to pacing.

Jenny's excited voice could be heard over the partitions. *We've got ourselves a winner at last,* Dave smiled to himself. *All I've got to do is give a nod of approval and we're off to the boat show!*

But Jenny wasn't coming out. He moved closer to listen, and his happy look turned quizzical. She wasn't talking about a suit; she was talking about *him*! Jenny was telling the salesperson the whole story of how she changed jobs so they could have their Saturdays together.

The significance of Jenny's job change sent Dave's mind into a bewildering whirl. *She went through all that just to be with me?* he asked himself. There was something in the tone of her voice that sounded almost sacred. He remembered other times when he had heard that same excitement and how he had squashed it when some change in his plans was required. A feeling of remorse swept over him as he replayed scenes from the past in his mind. She really hadn't deserved that kind of treatment, especially from someone who claimed to love her.

Tension that had mounted from falling behind in his predetermined schedule slowly began to dissipate. Dave felt relieved. He was happy that this day could be spent with Jenny — *his* Jenny, the one who made such great efforts to be with him. He smiled when he thought about how surprised she would be when he suggested her favorite lunch spot. Other ideas came to him that he knew would keep her spark of enthusiasm alive. He couldn't wait for her to come out.

❑ ❑ ❑

Momentum is as significant and valuable a factor in relationships as it is to a team trying to win a football game. It can be nurtured by a superabundance of enthusiasm, which quite simply begins by taking an interest in some idea, plan, or activity in which your spouse engages. The key to gaining interest is asking questions. The more time you spend trying to find out about your spouse, the more interest you will have. Genuine interest in your teammate is the rocket booster that launches Enthusiasm into orbit.

Ask questions until your interest is stimulated. Start with a two-minute series of questions pursuing an aspect of your spouse you know little about. As you gain more skill, see how many questions you can ask about one topic. Then observe the energized dynamics between you and your partner.

Enthusiasm is a by-product of our interest level and can help turn our marriages into winning combinations.

> *The Play: Daily express enthusiasm for your teammate's ideas and activities.*

Questions to Consider

1. What are ways in which you have dampened your spouse's spirit?

2. What areas of your marriage will benefit most from your expressed enthusiasm?

12

A TAP IN THE TUNNEL

More than one hundred thousand Michigan fans were singing "Hail to the Victor" as we walked down the tunnel toward the field. Our Minnesota team was playing Michigan at Ann Arbor—one of the oldest college football rivalries in college tradition. At stake was the winner's right to keep the historical Little Brown Jug in their trophy case until the next contest.

It was also my first start as a collegiate football player, and it couldn't have been in a more appropriate stadium. On autumn Saturday afternoons during my childhood I heard University of Minnesota football radio broadcasts booming throughout the neighborhood. I had acted out playing against the mighty Michigan Wolverines much of my youth, and now my dreams were about to become reality.

That year, Michigan was ranked as one of the best football teams in the country. Early in the first quarter, their fight song was echoing across the field. They scored, and scored again. It was looking like a rout.

Midway into the second quarter, we began a series on our thirty. We needed a big play. Our quarterback called a long bomb to me over the middle. I had to beat Michigan's safety, the All-American Tom Darden, which was no small task. He knew his position well, but what he didn't know was that in every childhood game I played against Michigan, I was the star.

At the snap of the ball, I took off like a shot for the goal-post. When I glanced up, I saw the ball coming down hard, directly out of the sun. My hands went skyward and I snatched the catch of a lifetime for a fifty-yard gain. Two plays later, I made a one-handed diving catch in the end zone and we were back in the football game. The half ended and we headed to the locker room. Though we were behind, we felt like we were holding our own against an excellent team.

As we walked down that long tunnel to start the second half, Coach Warmath tapped me on the back with his rolled up game plan. To a casual observer, his gesture may have seemed insignificant. But to me, it was an unforgettable moment. Coach Warmath knew how I had struggled my first year and a half through position changes and a broken wrist. To me his tap meant, "I believe in you. You're making contributions to our team. I'm proud to be associated with you. I didn't make a mistake by recruiting you. You have persevered successfully. Keep up the good work!" To this day the memory of his tap lifts my self-confidence and pushes me toward higher levels of achievement.

The Blessing of Affirmation

If you want to make someone's day, affirm something positive about their character. Let them know that you think highly of something they have done. Commend your spouse especially. Tell her what a good a teammate she is. Do it as creatively as you can. Genuine praise can uplift a disheartened spouse and change the course of a day. By affirming your mate, you'll take two positive steps toward a winning marriage. First, you'll make her feel good about herself and your marriage. Second, you'll avoid the bad relational plays that have kept your marriage in the losing column.

❏ ❏ ❏

"What a play!" boomed the game announcer. "Insult blitzed through the line untouched and put a tremendous hit on the quarterback! Oh, is he going to be sore tomorrow!"

"It's another case where the back should have picked up that blitz, Frank," the color commentator added.

While the crowd was chanting "Insult, Insult, Insult," Affirmation stood on the sidelines trying to figure out the chain of events that led to the midfield sack. He'd run his route perfectly and had been wide open in the flat. Why couldn't they ever get the ball to him? Affirmation didn't like the way his teammates were looking at him, as if it were his fault the play went bad.

He trotted back to the huddle. "What happened?" he asked innocently.

"Insult blitzed in here and said some terrible things that put our QB right on his back," his teammate responded indignantly.

"But I was open. The ball should have been thrown to me!" Affirmation shot back. "I mean, if you can't handle a blitzing linebacker by now you'd better get out of the game."

"You've got blitz responsibilities, stupid. You're supposed to check for the blitz before you flare in the flat."

"I did check. He wasn't coming that hard," he said defensively. Meanwhile, up in the press box . . .

"Okay everybody, we're back to the action. There's the snap. It's a hand-off to Affirmation and oh, low bridge! An absolutely stunning hit on Affirmation! He crumpled like a paper cup. How did he ever hang onto the ball? Who was that?"

"It was Insult again, Frank. It was almost like the line stepped aside to let him through. Monkey see, monkey do."

Affirmation lay gasping on the ground. "Cheap . . . shot," he said, struggling for breath.

❑ ❑ ❑

Roland looked at his watch. "She'll never get here," he said, perusing the concert program for the fifth time. The season ticket holders behind him were betting that she wouldn't get there until the first intermission. The orchestra quieted as their concertmaster walked briskly and confidently onto the stage. Hearty applause arose from the audience.

"Excuse me, excuse me . . . I'm sorry." Judy's singsong voice could be heard over the clapping as she stepped over some feet and onto others as if she were running the tire drill in training camp.

"Well, I'll be!" Roland heard the exclaim of the patrons behind him, and his neck reddened with exasperation. The season tickets had been her idea, but every month he had sat alone in the "Chair of Humiliation" while Judy knocked knees with nineteen no-nonsense people. Their seats were *exactly* in the middle of their row. *The least she could do was alternate entry sides*, he thought.

Judy sat down just as the conductor motioned his first downbeat. "Hi!" she whispered with a smile. She was obviously very proud of her timing.

That does it! If she thinks I'm going to take this humiliation one more time she's got another think coming, Roland thought, churning inside. It was bad enough that he had to tolerate classical music, let alone the stares of people in the vicinity. Judy was also looking at him. It was then that the noise from the program he was crumpling seeped into his consciousness. Rage pushed him into action. He angrily jerked his head down to whisper in her ear, slamming his nose into her raised elbow as she struggled to remove her coat.

Through gritted teeth he growled, "You are the worst thing that has ever happened to me."

As he settled back into his chair, his nose began throbbing to the steady beat of the timpani drums.

❏ ❏ ❏

Affirmation felt like his ribs were cracked. His teammate helped him to his feet. "You okay?"

He felt his side, stretched, and nodded.

"Once Insult has some success with the blitz, he'll keep trying it until you stop him. I know you can do it."

The encouragement felt good next to the ache his missed assignments had caused. He determined to watch Insult much more closely.

The next play was the same check/flare pass that he had missed previously. At the snap of the ball, Affirmation stepped up to take on the blitzing Insult. He was staying back.

Affirmation took a step downfield, keeping Insult within eyesight. "You rascal!" he yelled as Insult shot toward the quarterback. Affirmation planted his right foot and lunged at the speeding Insult, catching him on the hip with the top of his helmet. In an instant Insult was airborne. Affirmation then sprinted to the flat, took the floating pass over his shoulder, and turned upfield.

❏ ❏ ❏

Judy's whispered greeting was the last thing she said. As soon as the final strains of the first movement were swallowed by applause, she started to put on her coat.

"Where are you going," Roland asked quickly.

"To find someone who appreciates the incredible effort I made to get here." She bit her lip to fight back the tears.

Roland's mild concern about her departure had bought him only a few seconds. Having barely survived an intense three-day fight, he wasn't sure they could handle another one. He got up to accompany her.

"Let's go get something to drink. Why don't you leave your coat here?" He took her hand, releasing her fingers from their grip on the collar. He kept his hand on her elbow as they followed behind the others in their row.

"I'm sorry I said what I said. I didn't mean it," he softly said. "I know you have to get the babysitter and drive through a lot of traffic to meet me here when I don't have time to get home. I think you're a good mom, and you've worked hard to make sure we have this one special night a month."

Judy took a deep breath and relaxed her shoulders for the first time since the concert started. In the past, the angry incident would have kicked off a long term battle. This time, the right words sparked a delightful night instead of a three-day fight.

Affirmation: The Stuff of Life

Affirmations are written or spoken acknowledgments of another's positive traits or actions. They are blessings that warm a heart and bring on a smile. Affirmations uplift both giver and receiver. They make you want to redouble your marriage commitment. Affirmations given to your mate can overcome the destruction that insults have brought into your relationship. But for this transformation to occur, affirmations need to be as instinctive as insults have been in the past. This will take commitment to change on your part, and a lot of practice.

Typically, our offense of affirmation is impotent and lethargic from inactivity. All too quickly, we become defensive in our interactions with our mates, honing insults until they are razor sharp. But these expressions of anger only hurt our partners, and always bring further division.

But it isn't only anger that hurts. Insults masqueraded as humor can cause just as much injury. Teasing and joking with a sarcastic edge damage our teammates, too, particularly when these barbs touch sensitive issues.

The only solution in this destructive pattern is to create a new instinctive response. Affirmation must be practiced so that positive thoughts and phrases are consciously linked until they unconsciously become a part of your everyday speech.

You might be thinking, "Hey, if affirmation's not there, it's not there. Don't force it." If you applied that attitude to your work, you'd be looking for a new job. What you need to realize is that you've been practicing all along, except you've been practicing the wrong plays! You want to turn your team around, right? That's only possible if you regularly affirm your partner's abilities and actions. If you think she doesn't have anything to affirm, you make yourself look bad. She had enough going for her to attract you, didn't she? And if she lost something along the way, who took it?

When Debbie and I produced our first children's musical, "G.T. and the Halo Express," it was performed before some seven hundred ministers of music. We were nervous, to say the least. Since I had to be with the sound engineer in the back of the auditorium, we decided that Debbie should give the opening welcome.

She was very hesitant, and so I reminded Debbie of her experiences that qualified her to give the introduction. Naturally, she did a great job, and the production went beautifully. Afterward I quickly itemized five reasons why her presentation was so successful. The affirming boost helped restore her self-assurance, easing the taunting doubts in her mind.

In Dale Carnegie's book, *How To Win Friends And Influence People*, he emphasizes how important this affirmative approach is to success in relationships. He suggests that if we start each encounter with praise and honest appreciation, we'll gain the respect and attention we desire. It will also build up the other person's sense of value and self-worth. This is wonderful advice to implement in your daily encounters with your partner.

What You Can Do

Write down at least ten positive statements about your spouse and carry them with you. Repeat them several times daily to yourself, looking for opportunities to use them. Praise and honest appreciation are most effective when they come naturally in a conversational setting. As with everything, practice makes perfect.

If you suddenly start giving profuse affirmations your spouse will need a paramedic, so ease into it. The most important step is to make these affirmations a part of your language patterns. Remember that off-field practice determines on-field performance! But soon enough you'll be affirming your way to a winning marriage!

> *The Play:* Creatively and consistently affirm your spouse.

Questions to Consider

1. On the average, how many affirmations do you give your spouse per week? Do you think that's sufficient?

2. What do you think would happen if you gave her a minimum of ten honest affirmations every day? Do you think your relationship would change?

13

THE VICTORY CELEBRATION

My rookie year we played the defending Super Bowl champion Miami Dolphins in the next to last preseason game. They had won twenty-one games in a row, and we trailed most of the game. But with one minute left, we passed for a touchdown, making the score twenty-one to twenty in Miami's favor. We kicked off, and they had the ball on their twenty-yard line with fifty seconds remaining. It looked like a sure victory for the Dolphins. All they had to do was get a first down and run out the clock.

On their first play, quarterback Bob Griese threw a quick pass to Paul Warfield, who slipped a tackle and broke free up the sideline. The game was as good as over, and the Miami players began jumping victoriously on the field.

Now for the good part. Our cornerback sprinted from the opposite side of the field and made a last-ditch dive to stop Warfield. The ball was dislodged and then recovered by Jeff Siemon, our middle linebacker, who ran the ball back to Miami's thirty-five before he was tackled.

Our offense raced onto the field and ran a quick opener up the middle for ten yards. And then with two seconds left, Fred Cox kicked the game-winning field goal. We partied our way to the locker room while the Miami players stared in disbelief at the scoreboard.

Our team captain, Jim Marshall, later said that Miami was celebrating when they should have been playing. As a result, they lost the game.

Marriage Victory Celebrations

Sexual intimacy with your partner is one of the most exhilarating, relationship-building experiences you can have. It can also be a most demoralizing event that shakes the foundations of your relationship. Your choice of timing greatly influences which of these two outcomes will be experienced. And I'm not talking about the time of day or evening!

Husbands tend to view sexual intimacy as a *means* to building the relationship while wives consider it the *result* of a healthy marriage. She wants to celebrate *after* she feels secure in their relationship; he prefers it in the height of the contest. She wants affection that leads to intimacy; he desires intimacy which he believes is the same as affection.

These two differing approaches to sexual intimacy often lead to conflict. Resolving it need not be turned into a game of manipulation whereby "I give her what she wants and she gives me what I want." That merely keeps the relationship on a superficial level. Rather, we need to develop a keen sense of understanding our teammates before any semblance of a winning marriage can be established.

❑ ❑ ❑

"Indifference is having a field day, ladies and gentlemen! He's been all over the field making tackles and no one seems to be able to block him," said the game announcer.

"Right, Frank. Usually it's the fullback who's responsible for blocking the middle linebacker, but Affection's been just plain late getting there. For some reason he looks terribly slow today."

"It must be cold down there because he's got his hands stuck into his jersey. Sure can't catch a pass that way!"

The team was going nowhere. They were suffering a breakdown on just about every play they ran. Affection thought it was time to get the team energized.

"Hey guys, way to go!" he yelled as he came bounding into the huddle. "Let's celebrate! We're gonna beat these guys — all we have to do is get fired up! Come on, let's go!" Affection's cheerleading was met by incredulous stares.

"I hardly think this is the time or the place for a celebration," a teammate said disgustedly. "Why don't you channel some of that energy into blocking Indifference?"

❑ ❑ ❑

Mark walked through the kitchen without saying a word, though his newly purchased cologne left a tracking trail a mile long. He hoped Danielle would get the hint. She didn't. She stayed at the sink and finished loading the dishwasher.

"As if the dishes couldn't wait," Mark muttered as he picked up the newspaper. The Ann Landers column caught his eye. "Starved for Affection in L.A." the headline read. "Hmmm," he grunted. Danielle nearly choked when she smelled Mark's new cologne. "That's all he ever thinks about!" she said as she flipped the switch on the dishwasher. The familiar roar drowned out her comments.

"Hey, how 'bout you and me . . . " Mark began, flashing a surly smile.

"Sleeping in separate bedrooms," Danielle said, finishing his sentence. She picked up her book and headed upstairs.

Too much cologne for her, Mark thought.

❑ ❑ ❑

The hand-off sent Affection flying toward the outside.

"He's got a block and it's a race to turn the corner," said the announcer. "Indifference is closing fast and . . . oh, did you see that stiff-arm! Affection put a shot on Indifference's helmet and knocked him down to pick up another five yards. First down!"

"He finally did it, Frank. Affection took his hands out of his jersey and used them like a good running back should. That's the way ya gotta play if ya wanna gain yards in this league!"

It had been quite a few series since they had gained a first down. Affection was pleasantly surprised at how easy Indifference was to shove off. His confidence bolstered, he was ready for a field day.

❑ ❑ ❑

The Ann Landers column recounted the sounds and behaviors of a Los Angeles husband that could have also described a wild animal. Mark smiled. *His wife should have checked his species before she married him*, he quipped to himself. Rising to turn on the television, his accidental boar-like grunt and belch caught him by surprise. Usually he laughed at such grossness; now he was sobered by it. *Animal sounds. Not very funny.* The dishwasher kicked on, and he remembered the dinner he neither helped to prepare nor bothered to clean up. Come to think of it, he hadn't even said thank-you.

Mark walked over to the dishwasher and stood there for a moment. What had he looked like from Danielle's point of view? In his mind's eye, he saw a moose moving through the kitchen to plop down on the sofa, dropping hairs and leaving a sour smell in its path. *Not too attractive*, he thought. *No wonder Danielle's been so resistant to my advances.*

Mark reread the column and the letter writer's desire for affection with her animal-husband. She longed for the affection of face touching, hugging, and hand-holding. Mark put down the paper and looked at his hands. Then he looked at the dishwasher. "Time to shoot the moose," he said as he headed to the bathroom to wash off the cologne. If nothing else, he would at least give Danielle a hug and thank her for dinner.

The water on his hands reminded him again of the dishes he did not do. *Remarkable. Affection is related to the way I use my hands*, he thought.

❏ ❏ ❏

"THE ONLY TIME YOU TOUCH ME IS WHEN YOU WANT SEX!" This exclamation headlined today's opening of the Master Bedroom Convention in Walla Walla, Washington and was reported in the keynote address as one of the five most frequently heard sentences by walls. In addition, "Husbands are the Culprits" was the title of the paper presented by the panel that put the finger on married men from twenty to sixty years of age.

Walls from all over the United States and Canada were in attendance to hear keynote speakers Hi and Lois Walls, as well as attend other discussion groups. A few windows and doors were scattered throughout the assembly, dispelling rumors that it was a closed convention.

A banquet is planned tonight, highlighted by some off-the-wall entertainment from The Peels. (This article used by permission from the Walla Walla *Register*.)

A Legal Use of the Hands

Ignoring the emotional needs of our teammates while pushing for sexual intimacy is cruel and unusual punishment. True intimacy begins with hand-holding, walks together, gentle caresses, nonsexual pats, hugs, and loving words. You can learn many other ways through team meetings and study. Such loving acts are the nutrients that feed the emotional soul-needs of your partner. They are the plays that successfully move your team toward a winning marriage. Sexual intimacy is just like a victory celebration after a football game. It follows a series of successful rational encounters. That order must be maintained if a healthy and productive relationship between husband and wife is to develop.

Our partners will desire sexual intimacy if they feel affection from us. Affection is a primary reason our wives married us in the first place. Indifference to this desire will deter any progress you hope to make toward greater happiness together.

The Cold Water of Indifference

Symptoms of indifference include reading the newspaper while your partner is trying to talk to you. It's a noncommittal grunt in response to a question or a thought. It is a lack of enthusiastic interest in your partner and what she's thinking or doing. Indifference is ignoring her need to talk with you and be held by you.

Earlier you read about God's game plan where He told Eve that her primary focus would be her relationship with her husband. If our partners don't have a satisfactory relationship with us, their primary reason for marriage will be unfulfilled. Indifference to fulfilling our partner's primary reason for marriage, no matter what form it takes, will stop a winning team faster than a torrential rain shuts down a football game.

In a last ditch attempt to save their troubled marriages, many husbands will say to their teammates, "Look, do whatever you want. Whatever makes you happy. If you want to go back to work, fine. If you want to go back to school, fine. If you want to run for the political party leadership, fine. Don't even worry about what it costs." These "sacrifices" are perceived by some husbands to be the most loving, understanding, sympathetic, supportive action they can make. But it's really another way of saying, "I don't need you or want you around." It's not unlike a quarterback saying to his running back, "I'm going to run to the right. You can fake, go out for a pass, sit on the sidelines, or rest on this play. Whatever you feel like doing, just so you're happy." Such a quarterback is really communicating, "I don't want you in this play. I can do just fine without you."

The winning quarterback is involved with his teammates. Every play is purposefully focused to bring the team closer to its goal. He lets everyone know how important they are in the team's effort to win.

One of the very best ways of nurturing cohesiveness in marriage is through affection. Affection is genuine interest. It's looking into your teammate's eyes and smiling. It's a style of relating. It says, "I'm interested in you. I believe in you. I'm supportive of you. You are fascinating and very important to me." Affection is a relational play that will draw you closer to your goal of a winning marriage.

Affection's Two Parts

The affection play has two parts, verbal and physical. It's easiest to start by showing physical affection. Take your teammate by the hand. Run your fingers through her hair. Put your arms around her and hold her as long as she wants. Massage her back. Do this with *no* expectation of anything in return. It may take months for her to be able to believe you're not trying another ploy to get her into bed. You can really blow it here with a critical fumble, so get your mind straight before you start.

Also, say at least one affectionate thing to her every day. If you haven't been doing this, you may want to plan what you want to say. Write it down if you have to, but communicate from your heart. As you become more comfortable with verbal affection, your spontaneity will improve. As always, practice this play until it becomes natural and effortless. If you follow this game plan, your mate will be ready and eager to join you in a victory celebration!

> *The Play:* Express affection to your spouse in words and actions.

Questions to Consider

1. What are the ways you can express verbal affection to your spouse?

2. What impact would more affection have on your relationship? How do you think it would make your teammate feel?

14

HIDE 'N' SEEK

Being a rookie in the NFL was not easy. I felt young and out of place. It didn't help matters any that at every meal the veterans would ask one of the rookies to sing his alma mater while standing on the table with his hand over his heart. Since I was a home town boy, I was often singled out for fun. As I sang, the rest of the team would insult me, my school, my voice, and anything else that crossed their minds.

One evening when I was feeling down and lonely, several of the more fun-loving players invited me to join them for pizza after the evening meeting. I finally felt like I was gaining acceptance. After we ordered, they asked if I had any twenty dollar bills. I had two. They said I could play. Now that made me pretty excited, playing with the veterans. But I was curious. "Play what?" I asked. "Liar's Poker," came the reply.

The game had something to do with the serial numbers on each bill. We played the first round and somehow I lost, but I wasn't quite sure why. I lost the second round, too. I watched, dumbfounded, as *my* twenties were handed to the waitress when the pizza came. Suddenly it dawned on me that "Liar's Poker" was nothing more than a cover-up to get an unsuspecting rookie to pay the tab. I swallowed the bait—hook, line, and sinker.

Everything changed my second year. I was no longer a lowly rookie, but a player who was actively helping the Vikings win games. All cliques dissolved and interpersonal relationships deepened. I was part of the team and shared equal status with the most weathered vets. It was "all for one and one for all," a policy which was a contributing factor to our playing in the Super Bowl three years out of four.

Companionship Conveys Acceptance

The desire for companionship conveys acceptance because we spend time with those of whom we approve. I didn't understand much about companionship when we got married. For a long time I did my own thing, as if I were still single. I expected Debbie to live the same way. I was a lot like the fun-loving veterans, while she was the rookie looking for acceptance. Fortunately for me, Debbie persisted in her idea that marriage meant togetherness. By her sacrifices, she showed me what companionship really meant.

I felt this acceptance most from Debbie toward the end of my football career when I was hospitalized five days in the off-season for knee surgery. Debbie was student teaching at the time but spent every night beside me in a rather uncomfortable hospital chair. It was one of the most meaningful times of our marriage. Faced with the uncertainty of life after football, we discussed our options and how we felt about the future. The sacrifices she made to be my companion were great and made an indelible impression on me.

Knowing that she wanted to be with me made me feel more confident. I was an important person to her. I began to rely on the inner strength that came from her emotional support and just her *presence*. But it took some getting used to. At first, Debbie's desire for companionship was too much for me. I preferred my solitude and resisted her openness. She asked question after question when I'd return from practice, a speaking trip, or anywhere. She just wanted to feel like she'd been there with me. Eventually, my internal resistance to "being known" gave way when I realized the benefits of sharing time together. Only then did I see how much my efforts to avoid companionship had hurt us.

The Hide 'n' Seek Marriage

Adam had something to hide. He'd done something terribly wrong and didn't want to face the consequences. So when his Creator came looking for him, he stayed in the shadows. He would have gone deeper into the forest, but the compelling voice drew out his response. "I'm hiding because I'm naked," he said, his voice shaking like the leaves with which he'd covered himself.

His eyes had been opened with new knowledge about himself, and it was an uncomfortable feeling. Adam had disobeyed God's command, and with Eve, had eaten the forbidden fruit. He had quickly dismissed the option of confessing his wrongdoing. When he was confronted, he blamed Eve, the person formed from his own body. First he hid, and when discovered, he blamed someone else.

Just about every marriage book, manual, and counselor will identify the purposeful hiding of a husband's self as a formidable obstacle to a healthy marriage. Why we hide our feelings we can only guess. Maybe it's socialization. Many of us were taught to hold our feelings closely because expressing them was labeled as a sign of weakness. We'll avoid being vulnerable at all costs. It also could be that we realize we're not as strong as the image we try to present. And so we spend energy hiding our character flaws.

Husbands who emotionally hide themselves from their teammates collaborate with denial, indifference, and preoccupation to keep distance between them and their mates. When hiding doesn't work, husbands utilize demand, insult, and criticism to stiff-arm their wives, keeping *them* on the defensive. All of these mechanisms communicate rejection to our partners—rejection of their desire to be one with us as well as rejection of them as persons.

In essence, we do all the things that Adam did to defend himself. To screen his wrongdoing, Adam hid from God, then he blamed Eve. There's a remarkable symmetry between our interchange with God and our interchange with our teammates. We utilize the same opposing players to "protect" ourselves from both. The forces that fight against unity with our wives are the same forces that fight against unity with God.

The Great Mystery

In the New Testament, the Apostle Paul spoke of marriage as a great mystery. What is it about the dynamic of our relationship with our wives that is the mystery? Could it be that by working out a healthy relationship with our teammates, we are also opening ourselves up to a closer relationship with God? Could it be that in defeating the forces that oppose our marriage, we are defeating the forces that oppose the redemptive work of God in us?

Unlimited opportunities for growth are opened to us when we turn from hiding ourselves to following God's game plan for unity. Nurturing unity through companionship breaks the barriers between us and our teammates, thereby energizing the relationship.

I experienced this power my last year in football. After knee surgery, I signed with the Chicago Bears as they were looking for a tight end. Actually, the general manager was looking for a tight end. The coach was not, and it was apparent after the first day of practice that I would not be given a serious look.

I asked Debbie to come to training camp so we could be with each other. The truth was that I needed her emotional support. As a result, my football career ended on a happy note instead of a disappointing one. We left Chicago with great friends, warm memories, a new direction for our life together . . . and pregnant with our first child.

I'm thankful for that experience because it's a benchmark for how companionship changed a severe disappointment into a happy episode. Because of Debbie's support, I was able to avoid the depression that plagues so many professional athletes when they leave their sport.

The Simplicity of Being Together

There's no magic at all to companionship. It's just making plans to be with your teammate. You don't need to orchestrate a major event, either. It can be as simple as playing twenty questions. If your mate has tried to fill her life with other activities because of your past rejection, be patient. But be persistent. Go with her to her activities. And while being together, you can implement some winning plays that will hopefully reignite her desire for togetherness.

She may be suspicious of your efforts and look for an ulterior motive. That's why you'll need to have empty hands and an open heart when you're together. She must see that your motive is to reestablish togetherness and nothing else. In that moment, the mystery of marriage will begin to work again. You'll have made a giant step toward the kind of relationship God originally intended you to have.

The most important time to strive for companionship is when there's difficulty between you and your spouse. That's the greatest test of your commitment to a winning marriage and the time when your responses are scrutinized the most. By staying with your spouse during a disagreement, without hiding emotionally or withdrawing physically, she will feel more secure. You'll make a quantum leap in your relationship as a result.

How do you strive for companionship? Check your mate's activities calendar for opportunities to join her. Plan activities for yourselves that have her interests in mind. Take a walk together. Clean a closet together. Fold clothes together. Go for lunch. Play her favorite game with her. Watch the TV program she likes most. Get an ice cream cone. Make a two-minute phone date. The more creative you can be, the more she'll appreciate your efforts for a winning marriage.

> *The Play: Strive for companionship to establish unity.*

Questions for Thought

1. What circumstances are most likely to cause you to hide from your mate? How do you hide?

2. List the most significant deterrents for spending time with your spouse. Which ones can be changed?

15

"I CAN'T HEAR YOU!"

It was one of those Monday night games where the crowd was hyped for a home team victory. The only problem was that we weren't the home team. Atlanta was, and their fans wanted a win in the worst way. A win would secure the Falcons a play-off spot, which we had already attained. So the game was more crucial to them.

Jerry Burns had put a few new wrinkles into our offense to give our play-off opponents some additional formations for which they had to prepare. One of those formations had me playing as a split flanker. That put me about ten yards from the tackle, fourteen from the quarterback.

On the very first play I realized we had a serious problem. The crowd was yelling so loudly that I couldn't hear Fran's cadence or the snap count. Neither could some of the others on our offense. The roar was constant and deafening, as if we were standing next to a jet at take-off. Even when I moved back in to tight end I still couldn't hear. As a result, the timing of our plays was destroyed. We were hesitant going into our blocks, and Atlanta's defense continued to stop us at the line. The game turned into a punting war.

Sometime into the second quarter, Bud gathered the offense together and told us we would have to find a way to hear Fran, and that was all there was to it. By this time, the noise level had impaired my hearing to where I wasn't sure I could hear even if the crowd went home. But an amazing thing happened. I found that I could hear Fran if I concentrated solely on his voice. The first half, I had listened to the crowd. But the second half I listened for that singular and familiar voice calling out the signals. And I heard it through the roar—not because the fans were tired and the level had decreased, but because I'd focused my listening.

Crowd Noise in Marriage

Next to mules, husbands are the second worst group at listening. It's as if husbands are tuned to a frequency different from the signal given by their spouses. They have no trouble hearing spoken communication, but something happens to the words along their way to the brain. They often get scrambled, filtered, screened, and sidetracked. And so husbands respond by grunting, scratching, shaking their head, continuing to read, staring at the television, or walking out of the room without acknowledging that anything was even said. Such reactions trigger great frustration and anger in our spouses.

The problem is "crowd noise." Crowd noise may be a preoccupation with something else, disinterest in what's being said, or thinking of a response before your spouse completes her thought. Crowd noise prevents you from hearing your spouse and causes deep feelings of insecurity in any relationship. Have you ever spoken to someone at a public gathering, only to have them scanning the group for someone else to talk to? Remember how slighted you felt?

Or how about those who consistently interrupt your conversation with their responses. You feel like strangling them. They telegraph their disinterest in hearing what you have to say. As Solomon wrote, "He who answers before listening—that is his folly and his shame."

But listening can bring satisfaction and fulfillment that will carry over into every aspect of your life. The Scriptures indicate that places of honor and esteem await those who develop their listening skills. Good listeners can help to heal hurts, solve problems, and are regarded by others as wise. They will often rise to the top of their professions and experience success at every turn. "Let the wise listen and add to their learning . . . ." (Proverbs 1:5).

❑ ❑ ❑

Members of the media loved to discuss Listening's handicap. The fact that he wore a hearing aid and played football as a wide receiver seemed courageous. Phrases such as, "playing in his silent world," and "avoiding soundless tackles," were always used when his name appeared in the sports pages. He often said his impaired hearing was his best asset as a receiver because he never heard footsteps when a pass was coming to him.

Because of the attention his hearing aid brought him, Listening was given the coveted "Ear of the Year" award and invited to the White House. "Let's 'EAR It For Listening" posters were everywhere. Opportunities for product endorsements, speaking engagements, and public service commercials poured into the sports information director's office. Listening was a highly visible, sought after football player who became quite a celebrity.

But Listening lived in a mild but continuous state of fear that somebody might discover his secret: his hearing was perfect. The aids were simply a cover for ear plugs. He intensely disliked all the noise that enveloped a football game, and found the devices were a convenient way to disguise his synthetic sound stoppers.

There were other benefits besides the celebrity status. He didn't have to strive too hard for excellence because people didn't expect that much from a handicapped player. When Listening didn't want to talk with someone, he pretended to have trouble with his hearing aids, and they would eventually leave him alone. The only drawback was that when people did talk with him, they practically shouted.

All in all, Listening felt comfortable about the way his "handicap" had been getting him what he wanted. Life was a cruise and he was enjoying the passing scenery.

❏ ❏ ❏

"I can't understand it!" Wayne bellowed as he hung up the phone. "I work for a solid month to show those people just about every single house on the market, and they go and buy one from somebody else!" He stomped into the family room and threw himself on the sofa. "I hate people like that. No loyalty whatsoever!"

"I'm sorry they disappointed you, Wayne," Barbara said as soon as there was a pause in his outburst.

"I even showed them property across the river. They said they wanted something different, and there's plenty to choose from over there."

Barbara started to fold the laundry. She'd have to hear him out, just like she did all those previous times when he'd lost buyers. Real estate was tracking similar to other jobs Wayne had held. He followed a predictable pattern, starting to look for another "great opportunity" whenever disappointments mounted up. But the outcome was always the same — he struggled to keep clients. People just wouldn't put much confidence in him.

"I need to be in more of a business climate where people know how to act professionally," Wayne said with resolve in his voice.

"Did your buyers give you any indication why they bought their house from someone else?" Barbara asked. She was hoping he might discover some reason why these patterns kept recurring.

"Not really. They just talked a lot about fruit—something about seeing apples when they wanted to see oranges. I don't get it."

No, you don't, do you, Barbara thought, feeling anger well up inside. Wayne never could seem to understand what people wanted, let alone what she wanted. Whenever she tried to communicate with him, he would interrupt and start talking about something else. Barbara had to side with the "unloyal" couple. She wouldn't have bought a house from him, either.

❏ ❏ ❏

Soon after the "Let's 'Ear It For Listening" poster campaign was launched, Listening's self-imposed restriction began to limit his playing time. The quarterback could not call an audible when Listening was in the game because he couldn't guarantee the new play would be heard. The coaches stopped trying to instruct him in his pass routes because he kept fiddling with his hearing aids and they got tired of shouting. It had become too awkward to have Listening in the lineup, and so he was benched.

The more Listening reflected on his benching, the unhappier he felt. His synthetic sound-stopper solution had separated him from his teammates. *I've handicapped myself in the worst way,* he said to himself as he watched his teammates take the field. *If I hadn't been so stupid I'd be out there playing right now.*

Gentle words floated into his head almost like a subconscious thought. "Listening, if you can hear me, come here." It sounded like the head coach's voice. Was it, or was he just imagining it? Listening sidled over to him and asked, "Did you say something, Coach?"

The look of compassion on the Coach's face got Listening's attention. He felt hopeful. "I want you to go in there and run Flanker Right, 87 X Curl. Tell the quarterback to look for you. Make sure you run your pattern deep enough for the first down."

As he ran onto the field, Listening took both hearing aids and plugs out of his ears and dropped them onto the field. His quarterback looked so astonished that Listening had to assure him not to worry.

The stadium sounds were so exhilarating that Listening leaped like a gazelle to the line of scrimmage. For the first time, he followed the rhythm of the snap count. He shot past a shocked Preoccupation, whose defensive reaction appeared like slow motion. As Listening passed the first down marker, he curled back toward the quarterback, only to find Preoccupation in his face.

"Jump!" came the command from his coach on the sidelines. Listening jumped and saw the ball floating high and to his left. He tipped it, but was immediately hit by Preoccupation.

"Look up, look up," his teammates yelled frantically. Like a graceful ballet dancer, he reached to the heavens and plucked the ball out of the air just before being crashed to the ground. It was the catch of a lifetime and a critical first down. But more than that, it was an experience that started him down the road to true greatness.

From that moment on, he worked hard and caught up on the coaching he had missed. The clear new sounds he heard gave him a vibrancy for living. Listening even welcomed all who came to talk with him. He was determined to prove he was worthy of the "Ear of the Year" award after all.

❏ ❏ ❏

Within a few days Wayne had arranged an interview with a computer company for a sales position. Upon arriving, he was greeted by a very gracious personnel director who seemed quite interested in him. He wasn't asked about his work history, sales record, or education. Instead, the interviewer concentrated on his family, personal interests, and goals.

Wayne was amazed at how comfortable he felt during the session. His interviewer repeated the main points of each response before asking another related question. Afterward, Wayne asked for a cassette of their hour together because he felt he had really expressed himself well.

As he drove toward his real estate office, Wayne replayed the tape of his interview. He was surprised to discover that he was listening more for the interviewer's voice than his own. *He'd be super in real estate,* Wayne thought. And that's when it hit him. The interviewer would be good at anything because of how comfortable he made others feel.

A phone message awaited him at the office. *What a perfect opportunity to try out this listen-and-repeat stuff,* Wayne smiled as he dialed the client's number. It took him only three minutes to be convinced he was onto something big. He could sense the growing excitement in his client couple's voices as he repeated back their "wish list" of amenities before asking more questions. As the conversation continued, he became more conscious of hearing what his clients had to say. And he waited until they were completely finished before responding.

After many questions, the couple couldn't wait to meet with Wayne to see the properties he had described. They seemed to fit their needs perfectly. "You really listen to us!" they said as Wayne confirmed their showing time for late that afternoon.

"Oh, it's a new little habit," Wayne responded with a smile as he closed the conversation. He couldn't wait to tell Barbara. But on second thought, he decided to wait. He'd practice on her for a few days and see if she noticed anything. Somehow he knew she'd notice right away.

Developing the Listening Skill

When we fail to listen, we leave our spouses feeling like they've been stiff-armed. It's a nonverbal signal that their thoughts and opinions aren't valued. Thus, their self-worth takes a nose dive.

Too many times we try to educate our spouse: "That's not the way to think! This is!" Or we threaten them with, "If you don't want to change your mind, maybe I'll have to!" Sometimes we analyze them by saying: "You just think that because your dad always said that!" Most often we just offer a careless shrug or change the subject.

We think we know what our partners will say even before they say it. Our automatic responses then trigger the chain of events that lead us to yet another damaging argument that resolves nothing. *Skilled listening can circumvent these destructive cycles so that you can experience some healing in your relationship.* Here's how they do it in football, and how you can do it to help save your marriage.

Throwing the ball out of bounds is a specific play the quarterback makes when the play he has called goes bad and he wants to stop the clock. The infamous drive that gave the San Francisco 49er's the Super Bowl XXIII Vince Lombardi Trophy would have ended differently had Joe Montana not stopped the clock by throwing the ball out of bounds. Rather than risk an interception or take a loss that used valuable time, Montana utilized this play.

The philosophy behind throwing the ball out of bounds is that if you can't see clearly to make a play, don't make it. That also makes sense in marriage. Let's say you and your wife are discussing a regular problem, and she tries to get you to see things from her perspective. But you just can't for the life of you. The best thing to do is stop the play by throwing the ball out of bounds. Here's how you do it.

Make it clear with your words and tone of voice that you *want* to understand her point, but can't — not unlike the quarterback who can't see the open receiver down field. Tell your teammate that you believe her, believe *in* her, and love her, but at this time your vision (ability to see) is clouded. You want to understand and resolve the issue, but need more time. You may want to say that you're getting defensive and resistant, and you know that will only cause more problems. Also, express that you need to think through what she's saying, so you're going to write her thoughts down. You're doing this because you love her (and you do—it just doesn't feel that way at the moment).

Repeat what she is saying as you write down the issues. Make sure to write exactly what she dictates. And then set a specific time to discuss what you've written. Since you've bought some time by stopping the clock, study the sheet and try to feel her frustration and disappointment. Identify the obstacles that prevented you from listening to her. Then determine how you can make a successful play.

Fulfill your promise to your wife to talk about the issues. Sit across from her and repeat them point by point. Your goal is to make sure she knows that you're hearing her. By going through this process, your teammate will experience some relief in her frustration level because she'll feel that she's finally been heard. For extra points, take her hand as you talk together.

Doing this takes practice. You may not get it right away, and your teammate may be so frustrated with you that she explodes with impatience. But keep trying. Your only other choice is to keep getting sacked and throwing interceptions, and you know that only gets you farther in the hole. By unplugging your ears, you'll move toward a healthier relationship with your wife.

> *The Play:* To stop your argumentative cycles, discipline your listening to hear all that your teammate is saying.

Questions to Consider

1. What are your mate's recurring themes that you systematically tune out?

2. What response do you think your spouse will have if you follow the procedures in this chapter?

16

TEAM MEETINGS

As a football team we worked hard. But we also felt it was just as important to have fun. Often this was accomplished by schoolboy-like pranks. Our favorite target was our offensive coordinator, Jerry Burns, who at the time of this writing is the head coach of the Vikings. Since he constantly gave us grief, we felt he ought to take some, too. We tried to impress on him the importance of accepting our pranks graciously. This was so he would not upset the players and cause us to play even more hideous pranks on him.

Jerry's weakness was bugs and any other creeping thing. He *hated* them. From time to time we probed this chink in his armor. One rainy day at practice, I dropped an angle worm in the hood of Jerry's coat. Bud Grant saw what I did and walked over to Jerry. He just stood there for a minute. Then Bud shook a little and said, "Boy it's cold out here, isn't it?" Jerry promptly agreed and whipped his hood on. The worm slapped down over his forehead, and I thought he was going to die. He screamed violently while frantically trying to rip his coat off. You'd have thought he was covered with snakes!

Another day our All-Pro offensive guard, Ed White, showed up early for our team meeting. Upon arriving, he climbed a ladder and screwed a small hook into the ceiling just above the projector. He then attached a huge artificial spider to some monofilament line, running it down from the hook to where he sat, about three rows behind Jerry and to his right.

It was extremely difficult to keep a straight face during the meeting. Players kept snickering and Jerry would yell, "What's the matter with you guys today?" The more upset he got, the funnier the spider became. One player feigned a choking spell to cover his hysteria and left the room.

The lights were finally turned off and Jerry started the game films. The glow of the projector dimly lit the ceiling, and all eyes except Jerry's were on the spider. Even Bud watched the ceiling. Every time Ed jiggled the line, the spider would vibrate, sending waves of stifled laughter across the room. Steaming, Jerry raised his voice several decibels.

The spider was lowered little by little until it hung just above Jerry's forehead. He was staring intently at the screen, pointing out something about the way the defense would probably play us. Ed suddenly let the spider drop about an inch in front of his nose. Jerry completely lost it. He screamed, knocking over the table where the projector sat as he struggled to push his chair away. We were all rolling on the floor, except Bud. He stood with a straight face as if he knew nothing about the incident. In spite of Bud's demeanor, Jerry knew he was in on it. After that, Jerry was more subdued in films and kept looking over his shoulder. We had probed a little too far into his psyche.

The Agenda

Most of the time we were a well-mannered group of men who worked together to win football games. Much of this work was done in the team meetings. Besides reviewing films, we covered the previous day's practice, talked about the opposition, discussed new plays and how they fit into the game plan, and reviewed that day's practice schedule. The meetings were always well planned and orderly (for the most part). It was there that our offensive objectives were outlined in detail. We all shared an understanding of what it would take to win that week.

Team meetings are a must in football, as they are in marriage, if you're going to have a successful, winning team. It's at these meetings that you and your spouse talk about how you're playing together as a team, how the opposition has been stopping you, new plays that will help you win, and a practice schedule where those plays can be perfected. Such meetings are critical and should be implemented into your weekly schedule.

You can probably think of a hundred reasons why team meetings won't work in your marriage. Forget all the excuses and get on with it. To move you toward positive change, consider the following five ideas for your team meeting:

1. Team Meetings Should Be Scheduled Regularly.

One of the greatest gifts you can give your mate is to schedule *daily* time with her to talk about your relationship. Asking her how she feels about your marriage will give her 365 opportunities for expression in the coming year. That's probably 364 more than she had the previous year!

Make the appointment a priority, and schedule other activities around it. If it's not possible to make your regular time, then mutually agree to switch it. You acknowledge the importance of your relationship by the way you treat this appointment.

By having regularly scheduled meetings you convey your desire to stop losing and start winning. But when you first suggest this idea to her, make sure a paramedic is nearby. She may go into cardiac arrest!

2. Team Meetings Should Be Planned.

You've called the team meeting, so come with an agenda. This is not the time to say, "What do you want to talk about?" If you say this, you will have fumbled on your first attempt. Avoid making this kind of bad play.

Start with an introduction. You can discuss your desire to have a better relationship. You can say that you read about this team meeting idea in a book and are trying to follow the author's directions. You can express your hope that team meetings will improve your marriage. These are a few ideas to introduce the concept. Pick one and go with it. Above all, you want to obtain the interest and attention of your teammate. That may take ten minutes, or it may take one. But it's important to set the stage this way.

The next point on the agenda should be to pick something positive about your relationship to talk about. Express why you feel good about it, then ask for her input. If you strike a chord, keep asking questions to draw her out. *You need the information!*

Next, ask her to talk about a *specific* area of your relationship that concerns her. To her, all relational problems are connected. They are not isolated instances. She may touch on five or six areas, and that's okay. You've got to plan 365 meetings, and you can use her help with the agenda!

(I'd keep that paramedic nearby for your first meeting if I were you.)

3. Team Meetings Should Be Non-Contact, Non-Scrimmage Events.

These meetings are chalkboard sessions to discuss the plays that have caused recurring problems. So keep your shoulder pads and helmets tucked away. Remain objective and maintain an information-gathering attitude. A defensive posture can ruin your team meetings for a long time. Don't let a relational scrimmage materialize when your teammate expects something else. No surprise plays!

4. Team Meetings Should Be for Discussing Strategy.

There are plays your team performs well and those you perform poorly. You want to build on the good, improve on the poor. Your strategy sessions should involve discussions in both areas.

To qualify as a strategic session, your team needs to agree upon specific courses of action. One of the best ways to do this is to create a shared vision of a winning marriage with your mate. This is an activity you can start after you have established regular meetings.

Each of you should list as many descriptive sentences as possible that identify your idea of qualities that make a healthy, loving relationship. These qualities may or may not be those you already have working for you. Start each sentence with "We" and express the quality in a positive way. For example: "We are affectionate with each other," or "We are developing our individual talents." Don't use negative wording such as: "We're never affectionate," or "We don't help each other become better people."

After your lists are compiled, exchange and discuss them. Then combine the lists to create your joint vision for your marriage relationship.

When that master list is complete, place it in your home where you can see it several times a day. Discussion of the list and your progress on each item should be a regular part of your meetings.

5. Team Meetings Should Build Understanding.

Probing questions help build understanding and should therefore play a major role in team meetings. Your relationship may be plagued with vicious and destructive cycles which questions can help you to avoid. Ask questions and keep asking questions. If you get stuck or feel defensive, ask a question. It's one of the best ways to understand the viewpoint of your teammate and learn how she feels.

After your teammate has her feelings poured out to you, repeat them back to her. That will help her know you care and that she was heard. Anyone who shares their innermost thoughts and feelings will get upset if a response is not given.

❑ ❑ ❑

The idea of relational team meetings may seem impossible to implement, but they are an everyday necessity in a winning marriage. They are an offensive play designed to improve understanding between teammates. As understanding increases, so does unity in the marriage. But you must approach the exercise with sincerity and a desire to change. Team meetings are not an exercise in pacifying a teammate who wants to be heard. That motive will doom your meetings before they even start.

Several years ago, the sports pages were filled with news of the Vikings' worst season in years. They had hired a new coach who had instituted many reforms, some of which caused a lot of controversy. Whether or not the controversy was the cause of their losing record, no one can know. However, it was surely a major factor in the team's demise.

During this strained time, the new coach called a team meeting in which the players aired their frustrations. After the meeting, both the coach and player representatives talked with reporters. During the interview, the players reported that they had adequately expressed their concerns. The coach, however, reported that there were no problems on the team. The players were outraged to discover their frustrations had been so flagrantly discounted. In the weeks afterward, the team continued to lose, resulting in the coach's firing.

Don't make this mistake. Have *real* team meetings with *real* discussions about *real* issues. And create *real* solutions. Then you'll avoid the divisive destruction that criticism causes. And eliminating criticism from your repertoire of relational plays will automatically give you more yardage toward a winning marriage.

> *The Play:* To make positive change occur, have regular team meetings.

Questions to Consider

1. List three major deterrents to implementing team meetings in your home. What are ways you can overcome these obstacles?

2. Name some ways you can make your team meetings both fun and productive. Be creative.

17

A VETERAN'S LEGACY

Choosing players for a professional football team is a little like populating Noah's ark. You can only have so many of each kind on board. Teams usually carry three quarterbacks, five running backs, eight offensive linemen, four wide receivers, and two tight ends on their offensive unit. That's because the NFL limits the total number of active players. Keeping one more player in a certain position means you have to have one less player at some other position. In essence, making an NFL club is a numbers game.

When I was drafted by the Minnesota Vikings, they already had two veteran tight ends, John Beasley and Stu Voight. John "the Hoover" Beasley, who was nicknamed after the vacuum cleaner, had been the starter for several years. He maintained his image by catching everything thrown near him, and also by making vacuum cleaner noises during film sessions. His position seemed pretty secure, so I didn't think I had much chance of making the team.

Most rookies have major adjustments to make with the faster tempo in pro football. I was no exception. Everything was new and in high speed. The X's and O's that were so orderly and logical in the playbook seemed to blur on the practice field. I ran plays like a mechanical robot, hoping I could stay out of the way of the veterans who saw rookies as a threat to their jobs.

John Beasley was different. He didn't treat me like someone who was trying to take his job. After almost every pass play, John would tell me how I could run the route better. On running plays, he told me how to block specific players. He explained the blocking schemes so I could understand how my part fit into the whole. As a result, I played with greater authority and started to earn the respect of my teammates.

Helping a rookie was almost unheard of, let alone one vying for your position. John might have thought I didn't stand a chance to make the club, but I doubt it. One day I asked him why he'd been so helpful. He said he'd received a lot of help from other people and wanted to give back what he could. This isn't the kind of response you make movies about, but it sure made an impact on me.

Cooperation and Competition

John Beasley modeled a form of *"co-opetition,"* a healthy combination of helping me to do the best I could while performing at the highest level he could. He put the team's best interests ahead of his own. When the Vikings gave John his unconditional release about the fourth game of the season, I was pretty upset. His generous help that enabled me to develop as a tight end ultimately contributed to his release.

A few months later, after my first season ended, the Vikings selected a tight end in the third round of the NFL draft. I wish I could tell you I was anxious to "give back what I had been given," like my predecessor. But I wasn't so altruistic. My sense of security was attacked by the thought that someone would be competing for my position.

The receiving part of the "co-opetition" experience had been great, but the giving part was different. Now I was in John Beasley's place and had to decide in whose best interest I would act, mine or the team's. Being uncooperative with the new tight end would reflect poorly on me as a teammate. Yet being cooperative could cost me my job!

The competitive environment of football dictates that the spoils (the job, the money, the glory) go to the victor, and I wanted all I could get. If I hadn't cared about the benefits from playing with the Vikings, I wouldn't have been so intimidated by this new player.

Before you judge me too harshly, though, try to imagine yourself offering contacts, technology, and ideas that would help a co-worker replace you! Threatening, isn't it? Sharing helpful hints meant risking my position for the good of the team.

Cooperation is a key element present in every winning team. It's a highly visible characteristic in winning marriages, too. Couples who cooperate in decision making are happier and more productive than those who don't. That's why it's important for us to understand this conflict between cooperation and competition; it plays such a major role in the quality of our marriages. When we discover what hinders cooperation with our teammates, we've learned something valuable. Then we can avoid the disastrous effects that power-struggles have on our marriages.

Cooperation guarantees a balance of power in a husband/wife relationship. That's why husbands tend to be uncooperative in decision making. We're afraid of losing our power *in the relationship*. If we strive for power *with the relationship*, however, we'll have far greater success. We'll have the strengths of a team working for us.

There is much confusion about marital relationships, particularly on these issues of power and authority. Many husbands act as if there's only two rungs on the ladder of authority. The top rung, where they're totally in control; or the bottom rung, where they're a wimp. There is another rung — it's the place of give-and-take, where you're not measuring who's giving and who's taking. It's where the *relationship* has the power, and it's far more power than you can generate on your own. Let's examine some other models we have adopted for marriage that have caused us to miss the mark.

Common Marriage Models

Some adopt the model of the army general as their standard for marriage. Teammates and family are expected to follow explicit orders. Punishments are handed out for failure to comply. You can recognize this husband's wife by the bruise marks over her right eyebrow from saluting incessantly. This model allows no room for debate—it's his way or watch out.

Other husbands adopt a corporate model. They figure someone must have the final say—namely, whoever holds the highest position. Husbands generally like this model because it reinforces them as power broker. Corporate models are a little more civil than that of army generals, because they allow more room for discussion. Wives can submit their requests and can actually lobby for things they want.

Yet consensus in corporate decisions is more the norm than the exception, suggesting that a model requiring someone to "have the final say" is more theoretical than practical.

Both models are similar in their hierarchical design, and differ mainly in the degree to which they dominate.

The Meaning of Relationship

Throughout Scripture, God emphasizes unity within relationships. God's game plan calls for husbands to leave their fathers and mothers to be *united* with their wives, so becoming one flesh. Leaving and being united are action words encouraging us to move toward each other; toward interdependence and intimacy; toward mutually complementing each other. Marriage is a complete, interpersonal embrace between a man and a woman. It is not one dominating the other.

Unfortunately, we've lost sight of what God intended for marital relationships. Some have even defined marriage with rules, and feel that if we just follow them, we can eradicate all conflict. And the rules husbands all too often like are those that keep us in control of the relationship. Just as Adam pointed at Eve and said, "She made me do it," many husbands point at their wives and say, "She doesn't submit," as if the answer to improving their marriages is for the husband to usurp more power.

A New Commandment

Marriage was not designed after a corporate model; it was designed after God's own image where two people become one entity. And it is *the entity* that must have the power, not just part of the entity. For marriage to work after God's design, cooperation must be the predominant dynamic of the relationship. Agreement should precede action.

In talking about power and domination, Jesus said, "You know that those who are regarded as rulers of the Gentiles lord it over them, and their high officials exercise authority over them. Not so with you. Instead, whoever wants to become great among you must be your servant, and whoever wants to be first must be slave of all. For even the Son of Man did not come to be served, but to serve, and to give his life as a ransom for many" (Mark 10:42–45).

The Scriptural model for the husband/quarterback in marriage is not master over slave, general over field staff, chairman over the board of directors, or head coach over players. It is the model of a servant — one who sacrifices self-interest for the team's best interest. Interestingly enough, servants feel no need to defend their position. They have nothing to lose.

Refusing to dominate your household is not a sign of weakness, even if it seems to contradict everything you have been taught. Rather, it is a sign of strength. True servanthood indicates a complete dependence upon the Almighty. With His leadership, any house can be transformed into a home.

A Time for Reflection

It took a life-or-death situation to help me understand the importance of this model. Born with a serious congenital heart defect, our son, Barrett, needed extensive heart surgery to save his life. Doctors performed corrective closed heart surgery on him at fourteen days of age. Two days later, another complicated closed heart surgery was performed—designed to buy time so that Barrett could grow strong enough to survive the open heart repair he needed.

The risks were high. Barrett's defect was both rare and complex. The mortality rates for his surgery were extremely high. There were differences of opinion among leaders in the medical profession over which surgical procedures were best. Their differences fueled our indecision.

Yet we had to decide. Since I was always in a hurry to make decisions, I usually pushed Debbie into choices she wasn't ready to make. But this decision involved the life of our son. The wrong choice could end his life, as well as our marriage.

After many discussions, we agreed that we wouldn't commit Barrett to surgery until *both* of us felt it was the right time and we had selected the right surgeon. We felt some degree of peace that in our unity, we could better decipher God's plan.

After three and a half years of cooperation in data-gathering, consultations, and discussions, we made our decision. We committed to surgery. As a result of that extremely successful operation, Barrett is doing very well today. Abiding by this decision-making rule kept us from heartache and gave us great joy. Barrett's smile and hugs are an everyday reminder of the joys that can come through cooperation.

Even though competition between Debbie and I occasionally roughs us up and shakes our teeth, I have found that cooperation draws us closer to our goal of unity. Cooperation generates a spirit that can break down the walls of mistrust and build a winning marriage. It's a fail-safe play that *always* gains yardage.

How to Start

First, you need to know how you're going to cooperate. Here's some key questions to ask your spouse: "Is there anything I can help you accomplish today?" "How can we solve this together?" "How can we accomplish this together?" "How can we arrange our schedules so we can be together?" "Let's see if we can put our heads together to make this financial decision!"

Notice the key word: *together*. This is why she married you in the first place! She wants to be together with you in *everything*. And you know what? *You need her!* You need her thoughts, input, ideas, and abilities. You'll have your greatest success when you cooperate with her desire to be with you. It's the trademark of a winning marriage!

> *The Play:* Work toward cooperation and togetherness with your spouse.

Questions to Consider

1. What steps you are taking to become one with your teammate—one in concerns, ideas, language, time, goals, and in every area of your life?

2. How are you following Christ's admonition in Mark 10:42–45? How are you not following it?

18

THE POWER OF LOVE

Every Friday our Viking team spent fifteen to twenty minutes practicing our "red offense." That was the name given to the series of plays we ran in critical, short-yardage situations. The red offense was straight-on, block-and-tackle football, similar to the old single wing. The two ends were next to the tackles, the backs were in a "T" behind the quarterback, and the flanker was lined up one yard outside the tight end and one yard off the line of scrimmage. I was the flanker, and I both blocked and caught passes.

Our lead play was called "Thirty-Five Power," an off-tackle slant over a double team block. Once the first block was made, I was to roll off and slam the linebacker. My block created the hole through which our running back would explode.

Thirty-Five Power was the foundation of our short-yardage offense. We became very proficient at it because it consistently created a running lane for the back. If teams tried to compensate by loading their defense to my side, Fran would audible and we'd run to their weakness. We led the league in successful short-yardage conversions, and Thirty-Five Power was the reason why.

In my first play-off game, we were down by three points to the Washington Redskins late in the third quarter. It was fourth and one on the one-yard line. Our whole season was on the line. The play was Thirty-Five Power and everyone on the field knew it.

The defensive end and the linebacker dug in to fortify their resistance. At the snap of the ball, our tight end put a great post block on the defensive end. A split second later, I crashed into his side. He buckled under the pressure. Instinctively I shot toward the linebacker and saw stars as my helmet collided with his. The hit stopped him momentarily, then the avalanche of bodies buried him at the goal line. The crowd's explosive roar signalled we had scored the go-ahead touchdown.

I loved Thirty-Five Power! It was a great play because we could consistently crush the opposition's best effort to stop us.

"I Need That Play!"

I had to have a play like that for our marriage — a play that gave me confidence! I needed an action or a phrase that could stop an angry exchange in its tracks and result in a loving embrace. I'd try to be understanding when Debbie told me of her hurt. But as soon as I felt blamed, I'd slip into my armor and go to war with her. I needed a different response to unresolved conflicts that kept reigniting.

A few years ago, we attended a conference where we made friends with a couple named Dan and Judy. They had experienced trouble similar to ours in their marriage. We talked many hours about what they had done to bring about change in their relationship. But they had spent so much time and energy working through their pain that I grew discouraged. I concluded we'd always live with conflict. It was too much, too hard, and I just wanted to walk away. There was one story, however, that got my attention.

Dan said that after several years of marital turmoil and family havoc, he and Judy began long-term counseling sessions. As a result, he came to understand what Judy was seeking in their relationship. Over time, he realized that the "love" he thought he had given her wasn't love at all.

Dan's new insight compelled him to visit his father. On an evening walk, he said, "Dad, you've taught me many things that have benefited me greatly. From you I've learned how to fix things, the importance of reading, the value of hard work, and that anything worth doing is worth doing well. For all these lessons, I am very grateful.

"But in all you've taught me, there's one thing you neglected, Dad. *You didn't teach me how to love.* As a result, I've been sorely handicapped as a husband and a father."

Dan's profound yet tragic discovery that he wasn't taught how to love came almost too late in his life. But he forced himself to learn the lessons of love, and thereby restore relationships with his wife and children. It took time to learn how to respond to his children with interest and understanding. Concurrently, he had to discover that Judy wanted her feelings listened to, rather than "fixed." When he accepted responsibility for the hurt he had caused, he began to change.

Much like Dan, I had lived with the illusion that I was a loving husband. I, too, had fulfilled what I thought were my obligations. I was satisfied with my "performance." We had good-looking children, a comfortable house, nice cars, and close friends. But in trying to make the outside of our marriage look good, I had ignored the inside.

Looking at our marriage was like the telescopic glimpse I got into communist North Korea from Pamunjon, South Korea, the dividing point between the two countries. There I saw houses and buildings erected by the communists as a sign of prosperity to the democratic South Koreans. But the structures were simply empty two and three-sided shells without inner walls. They were just facades.

Just like the North Koreans, I had erected false fronts to convey the image that love was present in our marriage. I would say to Debbie, "I do love you, and here's proof. . . ." And then I talked about my specific acts of love as if they were supposed to satisfy the intense desire Debbie had for oneness. I thought love was what happened to me when I met Debbie. Unknowingly, I had put the full responsibility for love in our marriage on her. Now, many troubled years later, I was the one having to learn how!

Searching for Love

The night before a business trip, we decided to secure a cab to the airport for an early morning flight the next day. Cab drivers invariably came late to our house, losing their way in the winding streets that crisscross our neighborhood. Fortunately, our cab driver was on time, and we complimented him. In response he said, "The reason cabbies get lost isn't that they don't have a map. And it isn't because they don't look at their maps, because they do. Cabbies get lost because they don't know which direction is North, and without knowing which way to point their map it's as useless as the morning paper in getting their bearings."

I found the same to be true of love. If we don't know the direction from which love comes and point ourselves toward it, then all is lost — in our marriages and our lives. Even God's game plan for marriage can be misdirected unless it is pointed toward love. Virtue, confession, giving, enthusiasm, affirmation, affection, companionship, listening, understanding, and cooperation — they all work best when they emanate from love.

Just as the success of Thirty-Five Power was dependent upon the dynamic of two blockers merging at the point of attack, so the success of love is subject to the cohesiveness of two — you and the Giver of Love — merging to love your teammate. We cannot separate the gift of love from its Giver.

In the greatest directive ever given to husbands, the Apostle Paul wrote, "Husbands, love your wives, just as Christ loved the church and gave himself up for her . . . " (Ephesians 5:25). How could I love Debbie as Christ loved the church unless I had the very presence of Christ within me? God gave this overwhelming and all-encompassing commandment to me to achieve His divine purpose in our life together. Yet within myself I did not have the resources to follow this command! Upon asking Jesus Christ to enter my life, I had His limitless love within my being. Through Christ I had gained the ability to love in all circumstances. And change began to happen! Our "double-team" love began to reach out to Debbie's deepest hurts.

In the parable of the Good Samaritan, Jesus talked about a man who was robbed, beaten, and left half dead. A priest and a Levite passed by without helping him. But a Samaritan took pity on him and through great effort, restored him to health. I saw Debbie and myself in that parable. She was the one who was robbed, beaten, and left half dead. Like the priest and the Levite, I had left her by the side of the road. But her wounds needed to be cleansed and soothed. They required bandaging, and I was the only one who could do it.

In this ongoing healing and caring process, I've learned a special miracle of God's grace: that by loving Debbie, I am loving myself. When I give sacrificial Christ-like love to her, she is free to respond with genuine love and affection for me. The sacredness of our union is thereby recovered.

Even if your teammate's desire for you has turned to hatred, God's love through you can restore the love and respect that was so freely given when you were first married. It doesn't matter how much time it takes to regain those gentle feelings of tenderness toward each other. What matters is your willingness to love your spouse as Jesus Christ loves you. Only with His life-changing power can we hope to accomplish this divine directive.

The Power of One Play

Bud Grant used to tell our championship football teams that out of the 120 or so plays that comprise a game, there was always one play that determined its eventual outcome. One play changed the direction of the game and made the difference between winning and losing. We could win on the first play, or the last; but each play had the potential to bring victory to the team.

Each play directed by love can also make the difference for your marriage.

You'll undoubtedly be faced with the temptation to return to your old ways. But as you ask God for His grace, strength, and love, you'll be able to persevere to make each encounter with your teammate a loving one. Along the way loving acts will become so indelibly entrenched in you that they'll spill out to everyone who comes in contact with you, and you will be blessed as a result.

Implementing God's game plan for marriage will result in a loving relationship with your wife. And the healthiness of your God-inspired marriage will spill over into every other relationship you establish.

> *The Play: Humbly admit your lack of love, and ask the living Christ to enter your life to teach you how to love as He loves.*

Questions to Consider

1. Read and reread the Gospel of John and list the ways in which Jesus loves the Church. How can you implement these principles in your marriage?

2. Memorize Ephesians 5:25–33 so that it is indelibly imprinted on your mind. Think of ways you can love your spouse sacrificially, as Christ loves.

PART THREE
CONCLUSION

19

THE TWO-MINUTE OFFENSE AT WORK

Before a corporation adopts a new system, before a team installs a new offense, they want to know that the change will be successful. And you'll want some assurances that these plays will work for you, too! As the Apostle Peter wrote, "Above all, love each other deeply, because love covers over a multitude of sins" (see 1 Peter 4:8). If you're at all like me, you've got more unloving plays in your marriage game films than you care to remember. The *only* hope you have to restore the most important relationship of your life is to love, and love deeply.

I once told Debbie, "I'm going to love you today." It made such an impact that she asked if I would make that same promise my first communication to her every morning. It was a sincere request. That daily reaffirmation of my marriage vow struck a deep chord in her. It made her feel more secure, more valued. For me, the statement was (and is) an important reminder that my main business in life is learning how to love her more.

I clearly remember standing at the altar where we first said our vows. During that sacred part of the ceremony, I had an overwhelming sense that a heavenly presence had descended to witness our solemn exchange. Each time I tell

Debbie that I'm going to love her, I have a momentary reminder of that awareness. It reinforces that God is the coach of our marriage, and it is His game plan that I choose to follow.

Even when potential conflict swoops in on us like a fast-moving midsummer storm, I've been able to calm myself by seeing Debbie as my teammate. It's *our* problem rather than her problem. My participation in its resolution has dramatically increased our "successful solution percentage." We're learning how to shelter each other from the damage that the storms of conflict have caused in the past.

Instead of accusing each other of wrongdoing, we're identifiying the opposition that has kept our relationship locked in negative cyclical arguments. Once we identify the forces that try to separate us, we can release its positive counterpart — we can make a winning play that draws us closer together.

Putting It All Together

Just the other day I mistakenly threw away some papers that Debbie had purposely wanted to keep. To say that throwing the wrong things away has been an area of considerable conflict between us is an understatement! When she confronted me about the papers, I felt a middle linebacker-sized surge of defensiveness rising from my chest. In the past, I would have discounted the importance of the papers and excused my actions as harmless.

I started with my usual reactions, then remembered my Coach. If Debbie and I were on the same team, and the papers were important to her, then they were important to me. I admitted my wrongdoing and asked for her forgiveness. I affirmed that what was valuable to her was valuable to me, and if I had it to do over again I'd put the papers in a different place until she had time to file them. I offered to make calls to find copies. I wanted to do as much as I could to turn the situation around.

What has been an interesting observation is that the more I practice the two-minute offense, the more I value togetherness between us. I willingly give top priority to our relationship, because it benefits me! Does the two-minute offense really work? Yes! But only as it's practiced purposefully, followed carefully, and executed completely. It can't be sporadic. Loving our wives must be a moment-by-moment focus!

The Dream Is a Little Closer Now

It is possible for you and your teammate to move from a preoccupation with the hurts and details of the past to a warm and affectionate relationship with each other. Through commitment to God's game plan, love can become an automatic response. It can move freely between you and your spouse without any effort! Through the dynamic of your *relationship* you'll become a lighthouse of hope to other marriages treading through troubled waters.

I also believe that in the process of becoming real teammates you'll unlock the mystery of marriage. For the same forces that oppose unity with your wife — indifference, self-centeredness, lust, and pride — are the same forces that contend with God's purpose for you to become like Christ. Working for unity in your marriage will bring you closer to your Creator.

The influence of a winning marriage strengthens our children, because Scripture indicates that unity in marriage will impact their godliness (see Malachi 2:15). But the ripple effect doesn't stop there. It goes on to other marriages as well. I have observed couples whose living love is so attractive, so magnetic, that people will go to great lengths to be with them.

Jesus prayed for this kind of oneness in all believers, even as He and the Father were one. "May they be brought to complete unity to let the world know that you sent me and have loved them even as you have loved me" (John 17:23).

Others can judge whether Jesus was sent by God . . . based on our unity! Loving couples spreading God's good news are a powerful evangelistic force! Their influence has the potential to permeate their neighborhoods, places of work, and churches.

Husbands who love their wives as Christ loves the church — selflessly, without limit or reservation, with no expectation of returned love — will move toward God. They'll be victorious in fighting the forces that contend with God's work within them. They will be men actively doing the will of God.

The Clock Is Running

In the sixteen or so hours we are awake each day, there are 480 time periods of two-minutes each. That's almost five hundred chances a day to execute the winning plays in this book. You can have a fast start to a stronger, happier marriage, but you've got to get going! It's later than you think! The two-minute warning has sounded. The coach has given final instructions and sent you back on the field. The signal to start the clock is about to be given. There's a crowd cheering you on! You've got all the plays to quarterback your team to victory. Are you ready?

❏ ❏ ❏

"There's the snap. The clock is running. The quarterback drops back, and. . . ."

ABOUT THE AUTHOR

Doug Kingsriter was an All-American football player at the University of Minnesota. He was selected as one of the National Collegiate Athletic Association's Top Ten Scholar Athletes in 1973. Graduating with a degree in speech communications, he went on to be drafted by the Minnesota Vikings and played in Super Bowls VIII and IX.

Doug and his wife, Debbie, are the creators and producers of the popular children's audio cassette series *G. T. and the Halo Express*. They live in Minneapolis, Minnesota, with their two children, Lauren and Barrett.

The typeface for the text of this book is *Goudy Old Style*. Its creator, Frederic W. Goudy, was commissioned by American Type Founders Company to design a new Roman type face. Completed in 1915 and named Goudy Old Style, it was an instant bestseller. However, its designer had sold the design outright to the foundry, so when it became evident that additional versions would be needed to complete the family, the work was done by the foundry's own designer, Morris Benton. From the original design came seven additional weights and variants, all of which sold in great quantity. However, Goudy himself received no additional compensation for them. He later recounted a visit to the foundry with a group of printers, during which the guide stopped at one of the busy casting machines and stated, "Here's where Goudy goes down to posterity, while American Type Founders Company goes down to prosperity."

Substantive Editing:
S. Rickly Christian

Copy Editing:
Ann Hibbard

Cover Design:
Kent Puckett Associates, Atlanta, Georgia

Page Composition:
Xerox Ventura Publisher
Printware 720 IQ Laser Printer

Printing and Binding:
Maple-Vail Book Manufacturing Group,
York, Pennsylvania

Dust Jacket Printing:
Weber Graphics, Chicago, Illinois